Primary Engineering:

Projects for Grades K through 2

Terry Green
The Lincoln Public Schools

Foreword by Chris Rogers

College House Enterprises, LLC
Knoxville, Tennessee

The manuscript was prepared using Word 2002 with 14 point Times New Roman font. Publishing and Printing Inc., Knoxville, TN printed this book from pdf files.

College House Enterprises, LLC.
5713 Glen Cove Drive
Knoxville, TN 37919, U. S. A.
Phone and FAX (865) 947 6174
Email jwd@collegehousebooks.com
http://www.collegehousebooks.com

10 Digit ISBN 0-9792581-1-1
13 Digit ISBN-978-0-9792581-1-4

Foreword

As our world becomes more technologically dependent, we need to find ways to ensure that the average high school graduate understands the fundamentals of engineering. From global warming to acid rain, we have shown that our technological advances come at a cost and the voting public should have some understanding about how the engineers weigh these options in designing the technology of the future. The best way to learn this is to make these decisions themselves, as students, in a classroom. For the last 10 years, Terry has been leading a group of elementary school teachers at the Lincoln Public Schools to do just that. Where kids used to write reports on bats or spiders, they now build them instead. They navigate an artificial universe with their LEGO robots; excitedly learning and applying the scientific and mathematical knowledge to create, innovate, and build. By adding the hands-on engineering design process, Terry has gone from instructor to coach; her class has gone from quiet studying to loud discourse as groups discuss their designs. The major differences are in the children's increased excitement to learn.

I believe that one of the best examples of "technology in the classroom" is not a child sitting behind the computer monitor but rather a child that is up and active, with the technology simply a toolset that allows them to create and build. The 'technology" of my childhood was the woodshop—a place where we are allowed to make noise, try ideas, argue designs—a place where there was no "right answer" to the question the teacher posed. The woodshop is rapidly disappearing from the schools, and unfortunately with it goes the open-ended design and problem solving skills it affords. Terry's solution is to replace it by LEGO Engineering. Building with LEGO bricks is easy enough that children as young as 3 are able to create and build. LEGO Mindstorms adds the programming aspect, allowing the creations to move and react to their environment. When I visit Terry's class, I once again see the same excitement, discussion, and problem solving that were my favorite parts of my old woodshop class.

So how can you teach children to frame a question, brainstorm on design solutions, pick and test a solution and then iterate on the design? How can you get a 7 year old excited to learn about gearing? How can you get them to transfer this newfound knowledge to new situations and in new domains? Terry has successfully done this though presenting the students with numerous engineering challenges. By challenging them to build a snowplow that will move packing peanuts, she gets them to see why they want to learn about gearing. By having them build a wall that does not break, she has them thinking about structural integrity.

Terry has done a great job of pulling together a collection of the most successful activities she and other teachers have run in the Lincoln K-2 classrooms. From spinners to building chairs for stuffed animals, she presents examples where students build from directions or build from their own creativity. She also gives a structure for students to explain their design choices to the teacher—though an engineering journal. I hope her book will excite other teachers to bring more hands-on, open-ended design into their classroom. I hope more teachers will feel comfortable about teaching a subject with "no right answer". I hope that it will help more teachers learn how to become both instructor and mentor. I hope it will give teachers ideas of yet another way to teach the same concept in the classroom. Kids have many different ways of learning concepts; hopefully we can find many different ways of teaching them. Most of all, I hope that these activities will excite students to learn and innovate.

Chris Rogers

Preface

I wrote this book to help teachers who have no experience teaching engineering or using LEGO® building pieces as a teaching tool, but I hope experienced teachers find these lessons of value as well. Every one of these lessons has been used and tweaked over the ten years that I have been teaching engineering to kindergarten-through-fourth graders at the Lincoln Public Schools.

It may seem like a tremendously difficult task to teach engineering concepts to young elementary students, but it is a lot easier than you might think, and can be lots of fun as well. We think of engineering as a complicated and difficult realm of human endeavor, but first graders have no such preconceptions.

First of all, nearly every child has had some exposure to LEGO® pieces before they come to school. Because they think of LEGO® pieces as "toys," there is usually no built-in resistance to trying to use LEGO® pieces in a new and creative way. Motivating students to work on the lesson is rarely a problem. Most are eager to begin working with their materials almost immediately. The "tools" are familiar, yet are being applied in a way that the preschooler familiar with LEGO® pieces never imagined. It is as if the lessons are just the next LEGO® game.

The essence of engineering is using a defined set of resources to solve a particular problem. By framing these lessons as a simple-to-understand, but perhaps challenging problem to solve—such as building a car that goes *as slowly as possible*—the students wind up learning basic principles of engineering through their own direct experiences. The memory of these lessons stays with students for many years into the future, and provides a strong basis for future study of science and engineering.

Another benefit of young students having no preconceptions is the incredible creativity that is sometimes displayed. Since children have not yet accumulated enough life experiences to have "rational" expectations of what is possible, they can be incredibly creative in trying to solve the problems.

In fact, one of the strongest lessons I have learned in teaching this material is that there is no single "right" answer to solving the engineering problems that these lessons present to students. I am often pleasantly amazed and sometimes astounded at the types of ideas that young minds can dream up. Even when I think to myself, "that won't work," it is usually best to let the students learn that themselves. But sometimes, the very ideas I am biased to think won't work, actually wind up working! Alternatively, the "impossible" idea often leads the student to another, equally creative idea.

Unlike adults, young students are often capable of "thinking outside the box," because they have no established concept of where the "box" is. My one word of advice when using these lessons is not to let your concept of what is possible interfere with the student's creative process. You are likely to find that your students are far more creative than you are when working with these lessons to solve an "engineering" problem. I also suspect that seeing your student's creativity in action will be as personally rewarding for you as it has been for me.

Acknowledgements

I have many people to thank for inspiring, and helping me create this book. It would not have been possible without the creative, infectious enthusiasm of the students I teach. I am constantly amazed at the things they think up when solving problems and the ideas and solutions they teach me. They have taught me to be comfortable not knowing the answer and just letting the answer present itself though the engineering design process. I am also indebted to Chris and Cathy Rodgers for teaching me that young children can do engineering and are in fact excellent problem solvers. Chris first introduced me to the LEGO® pieces and ROBOLAB as a teaching tool many years ago. His enthusiasm, support and help over the years have made this book possible.

I also want to thank the people at the Center for Engineering Educational Outreach (CEEO) at Tufts University, in particular Merredith Portsmore and Elissa Milto, for their support in generating ideas and help in creating these lessons. I also want to thank Barbara Bratzel from The Shady Hill School for showing me what was possible and encouraging me to create this book. Her book *Physics by Design* was an inspiration and model for me. My thanks also go out to Eric Wang. His book, *Engineering with LEGO® Bricks and Robolab*, is an invaluable reference for me. Some of the photographs included in this book were from Eric's work, and I am grateful for his willingness to share them. Also, activities for Grade 1 Projects 3, 4, 8 and 9 and Grade 2 Projects 2, 3, 6, 9 and 12 are published with special permission from Tufts Center for Engineering Educational Outreach.

My colleagues at The Lincoln School have also been inspirational in helping brainstorm ideas and help test some lessons. I want to thank Gian Criscitiello, Sue Ann Kearns, Pate Pierson, Becky Eston, Rachel Scheff, Pat Hatsopoulos and Jennifer Leary. I am also thankful to my husband, Robert Green for his help in editing the lessons and my daughters, Katy, Ginger and Lucy for their support during this process.

Finally I want to thank Jim Dally for his enthusiasm and support in editing and publishing this book. He has kept the engineering accurate, improving each lesson with the correct engineering words and concepts and has been invaluable with editing each lesson.

Getting Started

About Primary Engineering

This book is divided into three grade levels, Kindergarten, Grade One and Grade Two, with appropriate projects designed and field tested for that age student. The projects assume a limited knowledge or experience using LEGO® building pieces both by the student and the teacher. The projects within a grade level build on each other. The knowledge and skills learned in an early project are used in subsequent ones. The students construct and expand an understanding of engineering, building techniques and problem solving as well as science concepts with each project.

The activities in the book use LEGO® building pieces, either DUPLO® in the Kindergarten projects or LEGO® in Grade One and Two. I list either the Mindstorm Kits or the Simple Machine Kits as materials needed but assorted collections of LEGOs can be used in many of the projects. In the projects that require motors to run, I list a battery pack (in the Simple Machine kit) or a RCX (in the Mindstorm kit) as the power source to run the motor. In the Grade Projects that require programming the RCX, I have included a section called Teacher's Programming Guide within the project description. Screenshots of sample programs and icons are included in those sections. The Teacher's Programming Guide has been written using ROBOLAB 2.5.4 with the RCX.

Each project is formatted in a similar way with the objective, time necessary to complete the project, materials, response sheets and vocabulary used. These sections are clearly labeled and the lists are bulleted. A detailed procedure or set of steps is written for the teacher to use to teach the project objective. Each project also has many pictures or sketches to help illustrate the concepts. Student recording sheets are formatted for easy copying for student use. Finally, each project has suggested extensions and appropriate assessments.

Classroom Management

Students are enthusiastic to use the LEGO® building blocks in a school setting. I usually group students into teams of two, or occasionally three, teammates. The projects assume the students will work as a team. This means working together, sharing ideas, creating sketches of building ideas and collaborating on building together in each project to produce a product or prototype. I usually require teams to discuss ideas and complete response sheets before any LEGO® pieces are distributed. Teams are asked to check in with the teacher before beginning to build. As building progresses during a project, I encourage students to stop periodically and observe what other teams are building. I call it shopping around the classroom. If a team likes an idea from another team, I suggest they borrow the idea and use it in their own design but make it their own by changing it in some way to make it better. Positive feedback is essential in creating an atmosphere of cooperation and collaboration within and between the teams. Students become teachers helping others with building tips. Competitive activities are discouraged while improving a team's performance is encouraged.

Materials Management and Storage

These projects assume the classroom has adequate LEGO® building pieces for teams to use in creatively planning and building their models and prototypes. Over the years I have amassed large quantities of LEGO® building pieces, both from the LEGO® kits I have purchased from the LEGO® Education Division and from donated pieces from the families of students in my school.

Management of LEGO® pieces can be a challenge! It is important to think what method works best for you and your classroom space. Consider easy access of the LEGO® materials, the successful building of the projects and the ease of clean up at the conclusion of the projects.

In my classroom I sort my LEGO® pieces into bins of like pieces rather then keep them in the original boxes (Fig. 1). I use the original LEGO® bins the pieces came in as storage containers. The bins are clearly labeled and stored in marked cupboards in my classroom, which are accessible to students. When projects are started, the teams are usually given trays or boxes to collect the pieces needed for the project. The LEGO® bins are removed from the cupboards and displayed in a central area of the classroom, with the bins labeled permitting easy access by the teams. LEGO® hoarding is discouraged and students are instructed to only take what they are really going to use for that class period. Pieces not used by a team are returned to the original bins and available to the teams during the next building period.

Fig. 1 Storage of LEGO® building pieces

I think it is important to instruct students on how to clean up and sort the LEGO® pieces into their correct bin at the end of a project. This skill is essential for the management of the LEGO® pieces and for peace of mind. The care used in cleaning up and sorting out the pieces from one project will be appreciated by the students in their next building project. I also have a "lost LEGO®" bin centrally located and clearly marked in my classroom for those pieces that end up on the floor (Fig. 2). Students are instructed to use this bin for pieces remaining after the LEGO® bins have been put away for the day. Periodically throughout the year I take ten minutes of a class and sort out lost pieces or check bins for incorrect pieces. This is a useful activity as the school year ends.

Fig. 2 Lost LEGO® piece bin

Additional resources

LEGO® engineering.com
> http://www.legoengineering.com/

A great web based resource for using LEGO® materials to teach engineering.

ROBOLAB@CEEO.
> http://www.ceeo.tufts.edu/

Another great website at Tufts University runs by the Center for Engineering Educational Outreach.

LEGO® Mindstorms Education
> http://www.lego.com/eng/education/mindstorms/

The official LEGO® Mindstorm site.

Physics by Design: Robolab Activities for the NXT and RCX, 2nd Edition by Barbara Bratzel is a great resource. It is intended for middle school students, and includes useful tips and engaging building and programming projects. It has great projects and experiments for different levels of Robolab and Physics.

Engineering with LEGO® Bricks and Robolab, 2nd and 3rd Editions by Eric Wang. This book is another great resource, written for older students, for building with LEGOs and programming in Robolab. It is an excellent reference for LEGO® and Robolab basics, including a detailed "Design Skill" section with tips and hints. It also includes excellent photographs describing methods to build various models and a troubleshooting appendix for the RCX and Robolab.

Contents

Grade

Kindergarten

Grade Kindergarten
Project One: Introduction to Engineering and LEGO® Building

Project Objective: To familiarized the students with engineering and working together on a team.

Time: One or two 45 minute classes

Materials:
- Assorted LEGO®/DUPLO® building pieces
- Read aloud from a book about engineers and what is engineering
- Small stuffed animals—1 per team (which is usually two students)
- Interactive whiteboard or easel mounted chart paper

Response Sheet:
- Recording My Science Observations

Vocabulary:
- Engineer
- Design
- Sturdy

Procedure:

The project begins with a teacher leading a discussion about engineering. The teacher may ask questions such as:

- Do you know anyone who is an engineer?
- What do you think an engineer does?

The teacher then discusses what engineers do, discussing different kinds of engineers such as structural, electrical, chemical, computer and mechanical. A read aloud story about engineering is interesting if an appropriate non-fiction book is available.

The students are presented with their first LEGO® challenge. To build a chair for a small stuffed animal. The teacher asks—what should be included in a chair? A list of requirements is written or drawn on an interactive whiteboard or chart paper for all to remember. The teacher directs a discussion about working as a team member. He/she then directs the students to design and build a chair for the stuffed animal, using ideas from both team members as they build.

When the task of building is complete, the teams bring their chairs and stuffed animals to the circle area for all to examine. The teacher encourages the teams to share their chair with the class, discussing what was easy or difficult to build.

If possible, the chairs should be displayed for the school community to view. The chairs can then be disassembled at a convenient time. Students will be instructed on the care of LEGO® materials and to sort and store these materials.

Assessment:

- Teacher observations and interviews
- Successful construction of the chair
- Completion of Response Sheet: Recording My Science Observations

Project Examples:

Bear in a large chair

Chair with legs

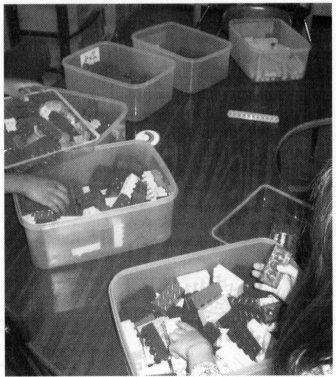

Bins used for gathering building pieces

Recording My Science Observations

Name: _____ **Date:**_____

Today, with a team, I designed and built a chair for a stuffed animal using LEGO® building blocks.

My picture:

My observations:

_____

_____

_____

_____

Grade Kindergarten
Project Two: Building with a Fixed Number of LEGO® Pieces

Project Objective: To learn the names of LEGO® pieces and then to build a free standing structure with a fixed number of these LEGO® pieces.

Time: One or two 45 minute classes

Materials:
- Assorted DUPLO®/LEGO® pieces, (sorted in advance into storage bins with the same type of pieces)
- Response Sheet: Recording My Science Observations
- Interactive whiteboard or easel mounted chart paper

Response Sheet:
- Recording My Science Observations
- My LEGO® Shopping List: Fixed Number of Pieces

Vocabulary:
- Beam
- Brick
- Baseplate
- Hub
- Axle
- Wheel
- Body Base

Procedure:

The project begins with the teacher leading a discussion reviewing the previous project about engineering and what an engineer does. The teacher then holds up a LEGO® beam (Fig. 1) and asks if anyone knows the name of the LEGO® piece.

Fig. 1 A 2 × 10 (two by ten) beam

He/she then introduces the piece as a two by ten beam and describes it as a building piece with holes in its side. The holes can hold other LEGO® pieces such as an axle. The teacher then draws and writes the information pertaining to the LEGO® piece such as a beam on an interactive whiteboard or chart paper. The teacher repeats this procedure with the other LEGO® pieces used in this project: Baseplate, Hub, Axle, Wheel, and Body Base.

The teacher then explains that they will be using these pieces to build a free standing structure out of a fixed number of pieces. They will only be allowed to use a certain number of LEGO® pieces but the team can build anything they like with these pieces. The team is to discuss what they want to build and then agree on a structure that involves everyone's idea.

The teacher then holds up a copy of the handout "My LEGO® Shopping List: Limited Number of Pieces" and explains that this is a list of the LEGO® pieces and the number of each piece they are allowed to take from the storage bins. The teacher demonstrates how to use the shopping list, gathering a few pieces, checking off the piece on the card and putting the piece in a bin. The teacher asks if there are any questions and then assigns the students to a team.

Each team is given a copy of the shopping list, a pencil and a bin to hold their pieces. They are instructed to gather their pieces, discuss their plans and build a structure. They are told how many minutes they have to work on the activity before they meet as a group and share their experiences.

Five minutes before the time for building expires, give the class a warning. When the building is completed, the teams bring their structures over to the circle area for all to examine. The teacher encourages the teams to share their structure with the class, talking about what was easy or difficult to build.

If possible, the structures should be displayed for the school community to view. The structures can then be disassembled at a convenient time. Students will be instructed on the care of LEGO® materials and to sort and store these materials.

Assessment:
- Teacher observations and interviews
- Successful construction of the structure
- Completion of Response Sheet: Recording My Science Observations

Project Examples:

My LEGO® Shopping List: Fixed Number of Pieces

Number needed	Part	√
1	6 × 12 Plate	
5	2 × 4 beam	
3	2 × 10 beam	
5	2 × 4 brick	
5	2 × 2 brick	
4	Tire	

4	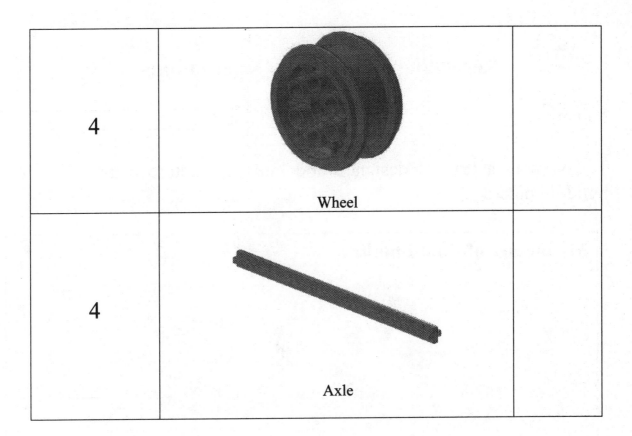Wheel	
4	Axle	

Recording My Science Observations

Name: _____ **Date:** _____

Today, with a team, I designed and built a structure using LEGO® building pieces.

My picture of what I built:

My observations:

_____

_____

_____

_____

Grade Kindergarten
Project Three: Spinners

Project Objective: To build a spinning structure using a building guide. The building guide can be a picture or drawing.

Time: One or two 45 minute classes

Materials:
- LEGO® DUPLO®: Early Simple Machines Set (**W779654**). This set can be purchased from LEGO® Educational Division at http://www.legoeducation.com. (The pieces should be sorted into storage bins with the same type of pieces before class).
- LEGO® DUPLO® Activity Card #9651, #5 from the Early Simple Machines Set
- Building Card "A Spinner", (A model built before class is used as an example)
- Interactive whiteboard or easel mounted chart paper

Response Sheet:
- Recording My Science Observations
- My LEGO® Shopping List: Spinners

Vocabulary:
- Spin
- Gear
- Tooth
- Crank
- Mesh
- Observation
- Template

Procedure:

The project begins with the teacher leading a discussion reviewing the previous project about names of LEGO® pieces and strategies for building strong structures. He/she posts the chart paper or saved page from the interactive whiteboard from the previous project with the picture and names of the LEGO® pieces.

The teacher then holds up a LEGO® 2 × 10 beam (Fig. 1) and ask if anyone remembers name of this LEGO® piece.

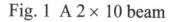

Fig. 1 A 2 × 10 beam

The teacher repeats this process with other pieces used in the last project. The teacher then introduces the new pieces used in this project, gear and crank, writing their names with pictures on an interactive whiteboard or on chart paper.

Fig. 2

Gear   Crank

The teacher explains that they will be using these pieces today to build a spinning structure, or a structure that twirls. He/she shows the students the model they will be building and asks them to make some observations about it. The teacher points to the gear and asks students to make some observations about the gear, asking how it differs from a wheel. The teacher introduces the word teeth and counts the number of teeth on the gear he/she is holding. Next the teacher shows the students how the teeth of two gears mesh and turn together. He/she introduces the word "mesh" and explains what it means and how to make gears mesh (Fig. 3).

The teacher shows the students the building card # 9651, #5 with the "The Spinner" and reviews the picture and some of the building tips students will need to consider as they build the spinner. The teacher holds up a copy of the handout "My LEGO® Shopping List: Spinners" and explains that this is a list of the

LEGO® pieces and the number of each piece they will need to build the spinner. The teacher reviews how to use the shopping list, gathering a few pieces, checking off the piece on the card and putting the piece into a bin. The teacher asks if there are any questions and then assigns the students to a team.

Fig. 3

Each team is given a copy of the shopping list, a pencil and a bin to hold their pieces. They are instructed how to gather their pieces, discuss their plans and build their spinner. The teams are told how many minutes they have to work on the activity before they meet as a group and share their experiences.

When the teams finish, the teacher gives them a copy of the circle template divided into 6 pie pieces and explains that they can color the parts of the circle different colors and attach it to the top of the gear to create a fun spinner. As groups finish with this they can be given the blank circles to create their own optical illusions, or eyes that will move or other creative ideas.

Five minutes before the time expires for building, the class is given a warning. When the building is complete, the teams bring spinners over to the circle area for all to examine. The teacher encourages the teams to share their spinners with the class, talking about what was easy or difficult to build.

If possible, the spinners should be displayed for the school community to view. The spinners can then be disassembled at a convenient time. Students will be instructed on the care of LEGO® materials and to sort and store these materials.

Assessment:

- Teacher observations and interviews
- Successful construction of the spinner
- Response Sheet: Recording My Science Observations

Project Examples:

My LEGO® Shopping List: Spinners

Number needed	Part	√
1	6 × 12 Plate	
2	2 × 10 beam	
2	2 × 4 beam	
2	Large gears	

2	Large axles	
1	Small axle with small gear	
1	Crank	

Recording My Science Observations

Name: _____ Date: _____

Today, with a team, I built a spinner.

My picture of what I built:

My observations:

_____

_____

_____

_____

Building Card: "A Spinner"

A template for making a spinner. Color each piece of pie. Tape it to the gear on the axle, and turn the crank.

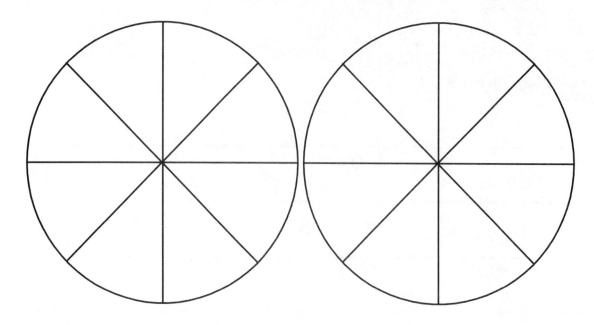

Grade Kindergarten
Project Four: Lifting a Load

Project Objective: To build a crane using a guide, picture or drawing.

Time: One to two 45 minute class periods

Materials:
- LEGO® DUPLO®: Early Simple Machines Set* **(W779654), This** set can be purchased from http://www.legoeducation.com. (Sort LEGO® pieces of the same type into bins before class).
- LEGO® DUPLO® Activity Card #9651, #4 from the Early Simple Machines Set
- Pictures of cranes provided by the teacher
- Plastic crane "buckets", which the teacher makes from cups and string
- Building Card "A Crane", (A model built before class is used as an example).
- Small objects (such as math manipulatives or pennies) to serve as weights to be lifted
- Interactive whiteboard or easel mounted chart paper

Response Sheet:
- Recording My Science Observations
- My LEGO® Shopping List: Lifting a Load

Vocabulary:
- Crane
- Pulley
- Load

Procedure:

The project begins with the teacher leading a discussion reviewing the previous project pertaining to the names of LEGO® pieces and strategies for building strong structures. He/she posts the chart paper or saved page from the interactive whiteboard from the previous projects with pictures and names of the LEGO® pieces. The teacher then hold up a LEGO® 2 × 10 beam and ask if anyone remembers name of the LEGO® piece. He/she repeats this with other pieces used in the previous projects.

The teacher then introduces the new piece used in this project, a pulley, writing its name with a picture on chart paper (Fig. 1).

Fig. 1

The class discusses what the pulley is and describes how it works.

Next, the teacher explains that they will be using these pieces today to build a crane. He/she shows the students the model they will be building and asks if anyone knows the name of this object. The class discusses where they have seen cranes and their uses. Pictures of cranes are introduced that demonstrate several applications.

The teachers shows the students building card # 9651, #4 with the "The Crane" and reviews the picture and some of the building tips that students will need to consider when they build the crane.

The teacher then holds up a copy of the handout "My LEGO® Shopping List: Lifting a Load" and explains that this is a list of the LEGO® pieces and the number of each piece they will need to build the crane. The teacher reviews how to use the shopping list, gathering a few pieces, checking off the piece on the card and putting the piece in a bin. The teacher asks if there are any questions and then assigns students to the teams.

Each team is given a copy of the shopping list, a pencil and a bin to hold their pieces. They are instructed to gather their pieces, discuss their plans and build a crane. When the teams finish, give them a bucket for the crane and explain that they can use the bucket and math manipulatives, pennies or other small objects from around the room to test their crane and lift loads.

Five minutes before the time expires for building, give the class a warning. When the building is complete, the teams bring cranes over to the circle area for all to examine. The teacher encourages the teams to share their cranes with the class, talking about what was easy or difficult to build.

If possible, the cranes should be displayed for the school community to view. The cranes can then be disassembled at a convenient time. Students will be instructed on the care of LEGO® materials and to sort and store these materials.

Assessment:

- Teacher observations and interviews
- Successful construction of the crane
- Response Sheet: Recording My Science Observations

My LEGO® Shopping List: Lifting a Load

Number needed	Part	√
1	6 × 12 Plate	
1	2 × 10 beam	
2	2× 4 brick	
2	Large arms	

4	Large axle	
5	Wheel	
3	Crank	
1	Pulley	

Recording My Science Observations

Name: _____ Date: _____

Today, with a team, I built a crane.

> **My picture of what I built:**
>
>

My observations:

_____

_____

_____

_____

Building Card: "A Crane"

Side view

Front view

Grade Kindergarten
Project Five: Balance

Project Objective: To build a balance using a guide or picture and to explore items that balance.

Time: One to two 45 minute classes

Materials:
- LEGO® DUPLO®: Early Simple Machines Set* (W779654). This set can be purchased from http://www.legoeducation.com. (Sort LEGO® pieces of similar types into bins before class)
- LEGO® DUPLO® Activity Card #9651, #2 from the Early Simple Machines Set
- Plastic crane "buckets", teacher made from cups and string
- Building Card "A Balance", (Prepare a model before class to use as an example)
- Interactive whiteboard or easel mounted chart paper

Response Sheet:
- Recording My Science Observations
- My LEGO® Shopping List: A Balance

Vocabulary:
- Balance

Procedure:

The project begins with a teacher leading a discussion reviewing the previous projects about names of LEGO® pieces and strategies for building strong structures. He/she posts the chart paper or saved page from the interactive whiteboard from the previous projects with the picture and names of the LEGO® pieces.

The teacher then explains that they will be using these pieces today to build a balance or seesaw. He/she shows the students the model they will be building and asks them to make some observations about it. The teacher introduces the word balance and discusses with the class what it means to balance something or to be balanced. The ideas discussed are listed on the chart paper or interactive whiteboard.

The teachers shows the students the building card # 9651, #2 with the "The Balance" and reviews the picture and some of the building tips students will need to consider as they build the balance. The teacher then holds up a copy of the handout "My LEGO® Shopping List: A Balance" and explains that this is a list of the LEGO® pieces and the number of each piece they will need to build it. The teacher reviews how to use the shopping list, gathering a few pieces, checking off the piece on the card and putting the piece into a bin. The teacher asks if there are any questions and then assigns the students to teams.

Each team is given a copy of the shopping list, a pencil and a bin to hold their pieces. They instructed to gather their pieces, discuss their plans and build a balance. They are told how many minutes they have to work before they meet as a group and share their experiences. As teams finish, after they have had time to explore their models, instruct each team to replace their LEGO® people with buckets that hang off the arm of each side of the balance. They will need to raise the balance up so it can swing freely. Building blocks or books work well for this activity. Place an object, such as a small block, into one of the pans and ask the teams to find things around the room that can balance the block. Next they can continue to explore objects in the room to see if they can find other things that will balance the block.

Five minutes before the time expires for building, give the class a warning. When the building is finished, the teams bring their balances over to the circle area for all to examine. The teacher encourages the teams to share their balances with the class, discuss what was easy or difficult to build. Next they should share the objects they used to balance the block and then discuss how they knew when the objects were balanced.

If possible, the balances should be displayed for the school community to view. The balances can then be disassembled at a convenient time. Students will be instructed on the care of LEGO® materials and to sort and store these materials.

Assessment:
- Teacher observations and interviews
- Successful construction of the balance
- Response Sheet: Recording My Science Observations

My LEGO® Shopping List: A Balance

Number needed	Part	√
1	6 × 12 Plate	
2	2 × 10 beams	
3	2 × 4 beams	
2	Wheels	

1	2 × 8 brick	
2	Base supports	
2	LEGO® people	
1	Axle	

Recording My Science Observations

Name: _____ Date: _____

Today, with a team, I built a balance.

My picture of what I balanced:

My observations:

_____

_____

_____

_____

_____

Building Card: "A Balance"

An idea for using the balance to compare the weight of objects found in the classroom:

Grade Kindergarten
Project Six: Catching the Wind

Project Objective: To design and build a rolling vehicle that moves by catching the wind.

Time: One to two 45 minute classes

Materials:
- LEGO® DUPLO®: Early Simple Machines Set* (W779654). This set can be purchased from http://www.legoeducation.com. (The pieces are sorted before class into bins with the same type of piece in each bin).
- Electrical box fan
- Assorted materials to be used as wind catchers: papers, tissue paper, foil, plastic wrap
- Assorted materials to be used for masts: Popsicle sticks, straws, chopsticks, etc.
- Clay
- Masking tape

Response Sheet:
- Recording My Science Observations
- My LEGO® Shopping List: Wind Catchers

Vocabulary:
- Wind

Procedure:

The project begins with a teacher leading a discussion about wind. The teacher asks questions about wind and records the student's ideas on chart paper. The teacher asks the students to think about things that catch the wind. He/she creates a list of the things the students identify. Next he/she directs a discussion about how the various objects on the list catch the wind.

The teacher then explains that they will be designing and building rolling wind catchers. The base of the wind catcher will be made out of DUPLO® blocks and wheels. The teacher shows the students the base and asks questions about how it is built. He/she shows the students the card "My DUPLO®/LEGO® Shopping

List: Wind Catchers" and reviews the names of the pieces. The teams will design something from these pieces to attach to their base to catch the wind.

The teacher reviews how to use the shopping list by gathering a few pieces, checking off the piece on the card and putting the piece in a bin. The teacher asks if there are any questions and then assigns each student to a team.

Each team is given a copy of the shopping list, a pencil and a bin to hold their pieces. They are instructed to gather their pieces, discuss their plans and build the wind catcher. They are told how many minutes they have to work on the activity before they meet as a group and share their experiences.

Five minutes before the time expires for building, the teacher gives the class a warning. When the building is completed, the teams bring their wind catchers over to the circle area for all to examine. The teacher encourages the teams to share their wind catchers with the class, talking about what was easy or difficult to build.

If possible, the wind catchers should be displayed for the school community to view. The wind catchers can then be disassembled at a convenient time. Students will be instructed on the care of LEGO® materials and to sort and store these materials.

Assessment:

- Teacher observations and interviews
- Successful construction of the wind catcher
- Response Sheet: Recording My Science Observations

My LEGO® Shopping List: Wind Catchers

Number needed	Part	√
4	2 × 10 beams	
2	2 × 4 bricks	
2	Large axles	
4	Tires	
4	Wheels	

Recording My Science Observations

Name: _____ Date: _____

Today, with a team, I built a rolling wind catcher.

My picture of what I built:

My observations:

_____

_____

_____

_____

Building Card: Base of Wind Catcher:

A sample Wind Catcher:

Testing the wind catcher.

Grade

One

Grade One
Project One: Introduction to LEGOs

Project Objective: To familiarize the students with specific LEGO® building pieces and LEGO® vocabulary.

Time: One 45 minute period

Materials:
- LEGO® Mindstorm or Simple Machine kits, with a tray of beams and bricks from Engineer Parts List (1 tray per team)
- Large laminated picture of LEGO® beams & bricks

Response Sheets:
- Engineer Parts List
- Assessment: ID the Part

Vocabulary:
- Bricks
- Beams
- Stud

Procedure:

The project begins with the teacher leading a discussion about engineering and LEGO® building pieces. The teacher asks questions such as:

- Who has played with LEGO® blocks before?
- What kinds of things have you built?
- What is fun about working with LEGO® blocks?
- Why do you think we are working with LEGO® blocks in school?
- Does anyone know an engineer?
- What do you think an engineer does?

The teacher introduces the two LEGO® pieces for the day—a brick and a beam. The teacher holds up a beam (a one by eight- beam; 1 × 8 beam, Fig. 1) and discusses the piece by asking probing questions.

Fig. 1

The teacher asks the students to make some observations about this piece. The teacher names the piece by calling it a beam. Beams are building pieces with holes in their sides. The teacher points out the holes in the side of the beam and asks the students to imagine the uses for the holes. The holes are used to connect the beam to other pieces and to hold axles (Fig. 2).

Fig. 2

The bumps on the beam are called **studs**. Studs help hold building pieces together. The teacher indicates that this piece is called a one by eight beam and asks the students why they think it is called by that name. LEGO® pieces are named by the type of building block and its size. The size is identified by counting the number of studs along its length and by the number of studs along its width. This beam has one stud along its short side (width) and eight studs along its long side (length) and is called a one by eight beam (Fig. 3).

8 studs along
its length

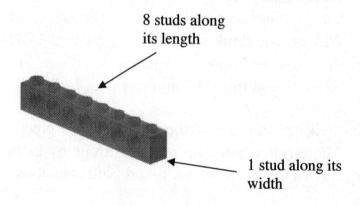

1 stud along its
width

Fig. 3

The teacher shows the students other beams from the LEGO® kit and identifies their size by counting the studs (Fig. 4).

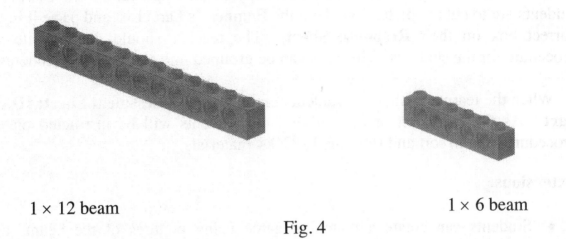

1 × 12 beam   1 × 6 beam

Fig. 4

Next the teacher introduces a brick (Fig. 5) and identifies the brick as a two by four brick.

2 × 4 brick   1 × 2 brick
Fig. 5   Fig. 6

The teacher asks the students to tell the differences between the beam and the brick. The brick has solid sides while the beam has holes in its side. The teacher holds up another brick (Fig. 6) asks the students to guess the size of this piece. It is called a one by two brick. The class then examines other bricks and guesses their size (Fig. 7).

2 × 6 brick   2 × 8 brick

Fig. 7

The students are then introduced to the project, which is to match the LEGO® brick or beam with its correct size. The teacher shows the class the tray of LEGO® pieces and gives each student a copy of the Engineer's Parts List. The students are to cut the picture out from the Engineer's Parts List and paste it in the correct box on their **Response Sheet**. The teacher should demonstrate the procedure for the students. The class can be grouped into teams of two students.

When the teams finish, each student completes the **Assessment Sheet: ID the Part**. As the final part of the activity, the students will be instructed on the procedure used to sort and store the LEGO® materials.

Extensions:

- Students can create a matching game using pictures of the beams and bricks
- Students can build a structure using the beams and bricks found on their tray
- Students can draw their structure on a sheet of paper

Assessment:

- Completion of the Response Sheet: Engineer's Journal
- Completion of Assessment: ID the Part
- Teacher observations and interviews

Response Sheet
Engineer's Parts List

Engineer: _____ Date: _____

Teammate(s): _____

Directions: Cut out the picture. Identify the piece and paste it into the correct box.

2 × 4 brick	1 × 8 beam
1 × 6 beam	1 × 2 beam
1 × 4 beam	1 × 2 brick
1 × 12 beam	1 × 10 beam

Engineer's Parts List

Directions:

Cut out each LEGO® piece.

Determine its name and size.

Glue it in the correct box on your paper.

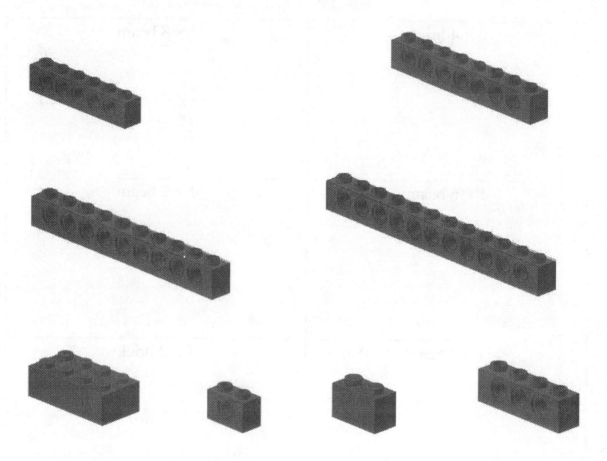

Response Sheet
Assessment: ID the Part

Engineer: _____ Date: _____

Directions: Cut out the picture of the LEGO® piece. Identify the piece and glue it into the correct box. If it is a beam or a brick, write its size next to the piece.

Beams

Bricks

Other LEGO® Pieces

Response Sheet
Assessment: ID the Part

Directions: Cut out the picture of the LEGO® piece. Identify the piece and paste it into the correct box. If it is a beam or a brick, write its size next to the piece.

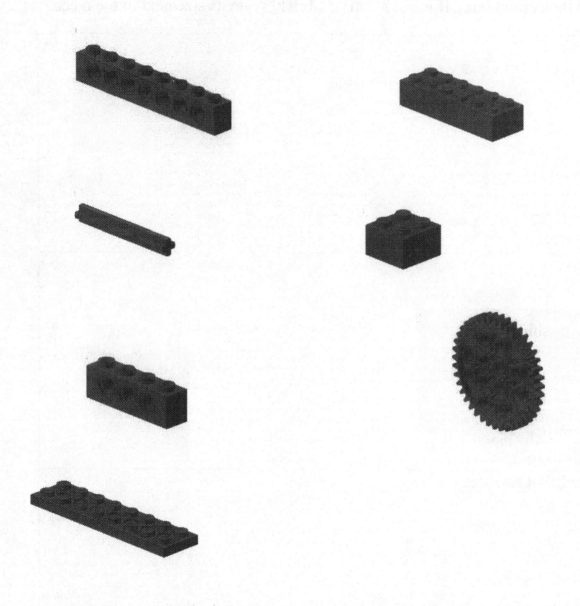

Grade One
Project Two: Introduction to Plates, Axles and Tires

Project Objective: To familiarize students with specific LEGO® building pieces and LEGO® vocabulary.

Time: One 45 minute period

Materials:
- LEGO® Mindstorm or Simple Machine kits
- Large laminated pictures of LEGO® plates, axles, hubs, tires, and bushings

Response Sheet:
- Assessment: Test Yourself
- Engineer's Journal

Vocabulary:
- Plate
- Axle (or shaft)
- Tire
- Hub
- Bushing

Procedure:

The project begins with a teacher leading a review of the LEGO® building pieces: bricks and beams. The teacher shows the class a beam and a brick (Fig. 1) and asks questions such as:

- Who remembers the name of this piece?
- What are the differences between these two pieces?
- How do we measure these pieces?

1 × 8 beam   2 × 6 brick

Fig. 1

The teacher introduces new LEGO® pieces: a plate, an axle (or shaft), a tire and hub, and a bushing. The teacher starts by displaying a plate, a one by eight-1 × 8 (Fig. 2), and discusses the piece by asking the students probing questions.

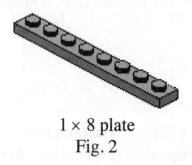

1 × 8 plate
Fig. 2

- What can you tell me about this piece?
- Why do you think a plate is called by that name?
- How is it different from a beam or a brick?

The teacher reviews the word **studs** with the students and names the piece. The piece is called a **plate.** There are plates with holes and plates without holes. This plate is too narrow for holes. The teacher tells the students that plates are measured the same way that beams or bricks are measured. This plate is called a one by eight. The teacher displays various plates and asks the students to give the size of each piece (Fig. 3).

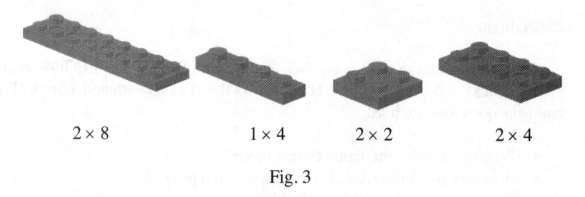

2 × 8   1 × 4   2 × 2   2 × 4

Fig. 3

The teacher introduces an **axle or a shaft** (Fig. 4) by asking questions such as:

Fig. 4

- Who has an idea of the name of this piece?
- What do you think it is used for?
- Describe its shape.

The teacher demonstrates that an axle or shaft is a rod that passes through the center of a wheel (Fig. 5). It can be used for many things when you are building with LEGO® blocks.

Fig. 5

The teacher asks the students to predict how they might measure an axle. An axle or shaft is measured by placing it next to a beam. If a beam is 4 studs long then the axle (shaft) is 4-stud long (Fig. 6).

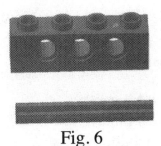

Fig. 6

The teacher introduces a **Tire** and a **Hub** (Fig. 7).

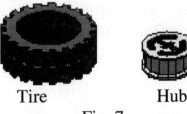

Tire   Hub

Fig. 7

Most children will recognize the tire. The plastic piece that goes inside the tire is called a **hub**. When placing the hub inside a tire the surface that is flush (tire and hub) goes towards the body of the car. The teacher discusses with the class when they might need a tire and how they might fit the axle into the hub.

Finally, the teacher introduces a **bushing** (Fig. 9). He/she asks questions such as:

Bushing   Bushing holding axle in place

Fig. 9

- What uses would be made of this piece in building with LEGO®s?
- Why would this piece be helpful?
- How could you use a bushing on a car?

The teacher then describes a bushing as a LEGO® piece that works like a stop (collar) to keep something in place (Fig. 9).

The class then takes a few minutes to review all of the pieces introduced thus far. The teacher asks the students to find specific pieces in their boxes and display them with questions such as:

- Can you find a 2 × 4 beam?
- Can you find a 1 × 8 plate?
- Show me a 12-stud axle.
- Hold up 2 bushings.

For the last part of class, the teacher groups the class into teams of two students. The teams are instructed to build something using only the pieces that have been introduced in Project One and Project Two.

- Beams
- Bricks
- Plates
- Axles
- Tires
- Hubs
- Bushings

When the teams have completed their building, the teams should share their structures and discuss a building tip they discovered. They are given the **Assessment Sheet: Test Yourself** at the conclusion of the project.

If possible, the structures should be displayed for the school community to view. The structures can then be disassembled at a convenient time. Students will be instructed on the care of LEGO® materials and on how to sort and store these materials.

Extensions:

- Teams can modify their structures to build a tall structure
- They can modify their structures to build a vehicle that moves

Assessment:

- Completion of the Response Sheet: Engineer's Journal
- Building a structure
- Teacher observations and interviews
- Completion of Assessment Sheet: Test Yourself

Sample Building Projects

Response Sheet
Engineer's Journal

Engineer: _____ Date: _____

Teammate: _____

1. Draw a picture of your structure.

```
┌─────────────────────────────────────────────────┐
│                                                   │
│                                                   │
│                                                   │
│                                                   │
│                                                   │
│                                                   │
│                                                   │
│                                                   │
│                                                   │
│                                                   │
│                                                   │
└─────────────────────────────────────────────────┘
```

2. Use this color key to color the specific LEGO® pieces on your picture. .

LEGO® piece on the picture	Use this color
Beams	Red
Bricks	Blue
Plates	Yellow
Axles	Orange
Tires	Black
Hubs	Green
Bushings	Purple

Response Sheet:
Assessment Sheet: Test Yourself

Engineer: _____ Date: _____

Directions: Examine each picture. Using the word bank, write the name of the piece on the line.

_____

_____

_____

_____

_____

_____

Word Bank

Axle
Bushing
Hub
1 × 4 Plate
2 × 6 Plate
Tire

Grade One
Project Three: Build a Sturdy Wall

Project Objective: To familiarize students with specific LEGO® building strategies and vocabulary.

Time: One 45 minute period

Materials:
- LEGO® Mindstorm or Simple Machine kits
- Large laminated pictures of LEGO® building pieces: beam, brick, plate, axle, tire, hub and bushing
- Cards with names of LEGO® building pieces (for matching with picture)
- Fictional book titled *The Three Little Pigs*

Response Sheet:
- Engineer's Journal
- Assessment: ID the Part

Vocabulary:
- Sturdy
- Overlapping
- Joint
- 'Flick test'

Procedure:

The teacher begins the project with a review of the building pieces used in the last two projects by playing a matching game, which entails matching LEGO® building pieces with their names. He/she also reviews the purpose of the different LEGO® building pieces.

The teacher introduces the project for the day by reading the story of the *Three Little Pigs*. He/she discusses the different techniques that the little pigs used when they built their individual houses. The teacher asks questions such as:

- What were the three materials used by the three pigs?
- Which materials were the strongest? Weakest?
- Why were the bricks the strongest?

The teacher asks if anyone knows the meaning of the word sturdy. He/she asks which of the pigs' houses was the sturdiest. The class discusses what makes something sturdy when they build with LEGO® pieces. The teacher shares some building tips with the class such as:

- Walls with overlapped beams and bricks are stronger than walls without overlapped beams and bricks (Fig. 1)

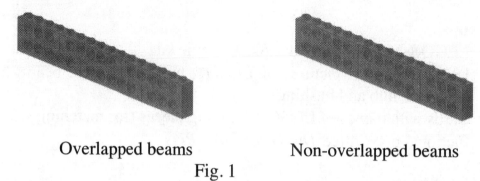

Overlapped beams   Non-overlapped beams

Fig. 1

- Plates can be stacked to make them the same height as a beam or a brick (Fig. 2)

Three stacked plates equal the height of one beam

Fig. 2

- Overlapping beams and bricks on the corners of wall or house make it stronger (Fig. 3)

Fig. 3

The teacher explains the building project for the day: to build a sturdy wall. The class discusses which LEGO® pieces they should use to build a wall (beams, bricks and plates) and how they can use the LEGO® pieces to make a sturdy wall (overlap the beams or bricks so the joints are staggered, (Fig. 1). The teacher defines the word joint for the students and the class discusses what a joint is on the structure and how to overlap the joints to make the structure stronger.

Next the class discusses how they will test the walls to determine if they are sturdy. The teacher introduces the "flick test", where the teacher uses his/her index finger to flick the wall. The teacher demonstrates the flick test on a wall for the class to observe and explains that their wall must be sturdy enough to withstand the flick test.

The class is divided into teams of two and the teams begin building their walls. The teacher circulates around the room, testing the walls and suggesting building ideas to the teams.

The class assembles together at the end of the period and shares their walls with their classmates. The teams demonstrate the sturdiness of their walls with the flick test and share their building strategies. The teacher should call attention to the way the walls in the classroom are constructed. After sharing the walls, the students complete the Response Sheet: **Engineer's Journal.**

If possible, the walls should be displayed for the school community to view. The walls can then be disassembled at a convenient time. Students will be instructed on the care of LEGO® materials and to sort and store these materials.

Extensions:

- Build a sturdy room that will withstand the 'drop test'. (This test involves dropping the structure from the knees of the teacher.)

Assessment:

- Completion of the Response Sheet: Engineer's Journal
- Teacher observations and interviews
- Building a sturdy wall that can withstand the flick test

Sample Building Projects

Response Sheet
Engineer's Journal

Engineer: _____ Date: _____

Teammate: _____

1. Draw a picture of your wall. Be certain to mark where the pieces overlap.

2. Write a sentence about how you made the wall sturdy.

_____

_____

_____

_____

_____

Response Sheet
Assessment

Engineer: _____ Date: _____

1. Look at the two pictures below. **Circle** the one which is the **sturdiest**. On the lines below the pictures, explain your answer.

Picture 1    Picture 2

_____

_____

_____

_____

2. Write a LEGO® building tip for another student to use about how to build a sturdy wall.

_____

_____

_____

_____

_____

Grade One
Project Four: Build a Chair for Mr. Bear

Project Objective: To build a sturdy structure, sized to fit a specific purpose.

Time: One 45 minute period

Materials:
- LEGO® Mindstorm or Simple Machine kits
- Fictional book: *Goldilocks and the Three Bears*
- A small stuffed bear about the size of a beanie baby

Response Sheets:
- Engineer's Journal

Vocabulary:
- Sturdy
- Overlapping
- Size
- Shape
- 'Drop Test'

Procedure:

The teacher begins the project reviewing the building strategies used in the previous project when building a sturdy wall. He/she shares some building tips with the class: overlapping beams and bricks are stronger than non-overlapping ones, plates can be stacked to make them the same height as a beam or brick, overlapping beams and bricks on the corners of house make it more rigid.

The teacher then reads, *Goldilocks and the Three Bears*. The class discusses what happened to Goldilocks when she sat in the three different chairs. The teacher asks which chair was the best for Goldilocks, discussing the attributes about the chair that made it better than the others for Goldilocks. The teacher points out the different chairs in the classroom and talks about the different features of each chair that make them sturdy and good for their purposes (small size for students, larger size for teacher, four legs, etc.).

The teacher holds up a small stuffed bear and asks the students to consider what size chair would be best for this bear. He/she explains the building project for the day: to build a sturdy chair for Mr. Bear using LEGO® pieces. The chair must be sturdy enough to be dropped and still keep its shape. The teacher introduces the 'drop test'. The chair must be sturdy enough to be dropped from the teacher's knees to the floor and not fall apart. The teacher demonstrates a 'drop test' to show the children what is expected. The teacher explains that the chair must be the correct size for Mr. Bear so that he is able to fit into it.

The class is divided into teams of two and begins designing and building their chairs. The teacher circulates around the room, testing the chairs with the drop test and suggesting ideas to the teams for improving their designs.

The class assembles at the end of the period to share their chairs. The teams should discuss some of the problems they encountered and the strategies they used to solve these problems. If possible, the teacher should call attention to the way the chairs in the classroom are constructed. After sharing their chairs, the students should complete the **Response Sheet: Engineer's Journal**.

If possible, the chairs should be displayed for the school community to view. The chairs can then be disassembled at a convenient time. Students will be instructed on the care of LEGO® materials and to sort and store these materials.

Extensions

- Build a top on the chair to provide shade for Mr. Bear
- Build a bed for Mr. Bear
- Build something special for Mr. Bear. It must be 'his size.

Assessment:

- Teacher observations and interviews
- Building of a sturdy, correctly sized chair
- Completion of the Engineer's Journal

Sample Building Projects

Response Sheet
Engineer's Journal

Engineer: _____ Date: _____

Teammate: _____

1. Draw a picture of your chair.

2. Write a sentence about how you made the chair sturdy and the correct size.

_____

_____

_____

_____

_____

Grade One
Project Five: Introduction to Gears

Project Objective: To build a sturdy gear box where many gears are utilized and every gear is driven from the same driver.

Time: One to two 45 minute periods

Materials:
- LEGO® Mindstorm or Simple Machine kits
- Large laminated picture of LEGO® gears
- Pictures/samples of examples of gears used in everyday things (old egg beaters, bicycles, drills, can openers)
- Simple gear box for demonstration

Response Sheet:
- Engineer's Journal
- Assessment: Gears

Vocabulary:
- Gear
- Tooth/teeth
- Driver
- Follower
- Mesh
- Sturdy
- Size
- Shape

Procedure:

The teacher begins the project reviewing the building strategies used in the previous projects. He/she shares some building tips with the class: overlapping beams and bricks are stronger than non-overlapping ones, plates can be stacked to make them the same height as a beam or brick, overlapping beams and bricks on the corners of structure make it stronger.

The teacher displays examples of common household objects with gears and asks the students if anyone knows the uses of the various objects. The teacher then identifies the objects and shows the students where the gears are located and models how the gears work.

The teacher displays a picture of an 8 tooth LEGO® gear (Fig. 1) and displays a gear for the class to observe. He/she asks the students to make some observations about the gear.

8 tooth spur gear
Fig. 1

The teacher then defines a gear as a special wheel with teeth. The teacher asks the class to count aloud the number of teeth on this gear. He/she then names the gear, an 8-tooth spur gear and demonstrates how to insert an axle into the gear (Fig. 2).

Axle inserted into gear   Axle-gear assembly inserted into wall
Fig. 2   Fig. 3

Using a simple gear wall, the teacher demonstrates how to insert an axle in the gear and place the axle through a hole in the gear wall (Fig. 3). The teacher shows the class and how to use a bushing to keep the gear in place. He/she discusses the importance of supporting the gears in the wall with the axles and bushings.

The teacher then holds up a twenty four-tooth spur gear and its picture (Fig. 4). The class then makes observations about the 24-tooth LEGO® gear. The teacher asks the class to determine the number of teeth on this gear by counting aloud with him or her. He/she names the gear, 24-tooth gear and puts and inserts an axle in its center hole.

24 tooth spur gear
Fig. 4

Meshed gears
Fig. 5

Next the teacher asks the class to predict what would happen if the two gears touched each other. He/she then demonstrates gear meshing on the gear box, and defines it what is meant when gears mesh (Fig. 5).

The teacher then asks the class to predict what would happen if he/she turns one of the meshed gears (it turns the other). The teacher inserts a crank into one of the gears and turns the gear for the class to observe (Fig. 6). The teacher tells the class the gear that initiates the movement is called the driver gear. The gear or gears that are moved by the driver are called the follower gear(s).

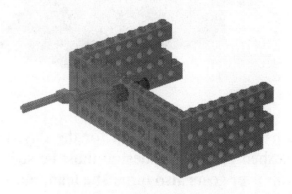

Fig. 6

The teacher introduces the 16 and 40 tooth LEGO® gears, counting the number of teeth and naming the gears. Next the teacher holds up a crown gear and shows its picture. The class is asked to makes observations pertaining top the 24 tooth crown gear (Fig. 7). The teacher asks the class to determine the number of teeth on this gear by counting aloud with him or her. He/she names the gear, 24-tooth crown gear and inserts an axle in its center hole.

Fig. 7

The teacher demonstrates how to mesh a spur gear with a crown gear and points out that the crown gear changes the orientation of the axles (Fig. 8). (Note: this concept is explored in depth in the Grade 2 project on crown gears)

Fig, 8

The teacher explains the building project for the day: to build a sturdy gear box, with at least 5 meshed gears. The design must be such that when the driver gear turns, all of the follower gears also turn. The team must first build a gear box that is sturdy enough to survive the drop test, from knee height and still keep its shape.

The class is divided into teams of two teammates and begins building their gear boxes. The teacher circulates around the class, testing the gear boxes with the drop test and suggesting ideas for improving their designs to the teams.

The class assembles at the end of the period to share their gear boxes with their classmates. The teams should name their gear box and share some of the problems they encountered as they built it. They should also describe the strategies they used to solve their problems. The teacher should call attention to the building techniques used in constructing the gear boxes. After sharing the gear boxes, the students should complete the **Response Sheet: Engineer's Journal**. Students should complete the **Response Sheet: Assessment: Gears.**

If possible, the gear boxes should be displayed for the school community to view. The gear boxes can then be disassembled at a convenient time. Students will be instructed on the care of LEGO® materials and to sort and store these materials.

Extensions:

- Add 5 more meshed gears to the gear box.
- Build a gear box where the last follower gear goes faster than the driver.
- Build a gear box where the last follower gear goes slower than the driver.
- Reverse engineer an old, broken piece of machinery by taking it apart.

Assessment:

- Teacher's observations and interviews
- Building of a sturdy, gear box with at least 5 meshed gears
- Completion of the Response Sheet: Engineer's Journal
- Completion of the Response Sheet: Assessment: Gears

Sample Building Projects

Simple Gearbox

Complex Gearbox

Complex gearbox

Response Sheet
Engineer's Journal

Engineer: _____ Date: _____

Teammate: _____

Name of Gear Box: _____

1. Draw a picture of your gear box.

2. Write a sentence about how you made the gear box.

_____

_____

_____

_____

_____

Response Sheet
Assessment: Gears

Engineer: _____ Date: _____

Count the number of teeth on each gear. Write the number on the line in the box.

_____

_____

_____

_____

LEGO® Gears to enlarge and laminate:

	8 tooth spur gear
	16 tooth spur gear
	24 tooth spur gear
	40 tooth spur gear

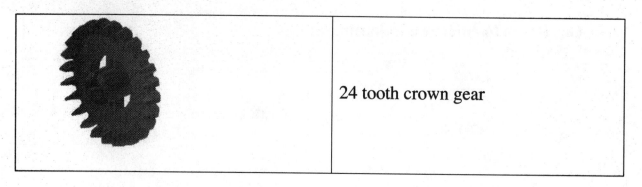	24 tooth crown gear

Background information:

Other gears in LEGO® kits

	Bevel gear
	Rack gear
	Screw of worm gear pair
	Gear box

Grade One
Project Six: Introduction to Pulleys

Project Objective: To build a sturdy pulley wall.

Time: One to two 45 minute periods

Materials:
- LEGO® Mindstorm or Simple Machine kits
- Pictures/samples of pulleys used in everyday things (Flag pole, clothesline, fishing rod)
- Simple pulley wall for demonstration

Response Sheet:
- Engineer's Journal
- Assessment: Pulleys

Vocabulary:
- Pulley
- Belts
- Driver
- Follower
- Belt Tension
- Slip
- Sturdy
- Size

Procedure:

The teacher displays pictures or examples of pulleys and asks the students if anyone knows the uses made of the various objects. The teacher then identifies the objects and shows the students where the pulleys are located. The teacher then holds up three LEGO® pulley wheels for the class to observe (Fig. 1). He/she defines the pulley wheel as a wheel with a groove which can hold a pulley belt and demonstrates where the groove is located on each of the pulley wheels.

Small pulley   Pulley wheel   Large Pulley wheel
                        Fig. 1

He/she asks the students to make some observations about the pulleys, asking probing questions such as:

- Where have you seen a device like this?
- What does a pulley do?
- Why were they invented?
- Are they always the same size and shape?
- What makes one pulley turn another pulley?

The teacher demonstrates how to insert an axle in one of the pulleys (Fig. 2).

Pulley with axle
Fig. 2

He/she demonstrates attaching the pulley to the pulley wall, securing the axle to the wall with a bushing. The teacher repeats the demonstration for the second pulley (Fig. 3). The teacher connects the two pulleys using a pulley band or belt. He/she describes the belt tension to the class as a pulling force by the pulley belt in the groove of each pulley wheel. He/she asks the students how they might change or adjust the tension if it is too tight (move the pulleys closer together) or too loose (move the pulleys farther apart).

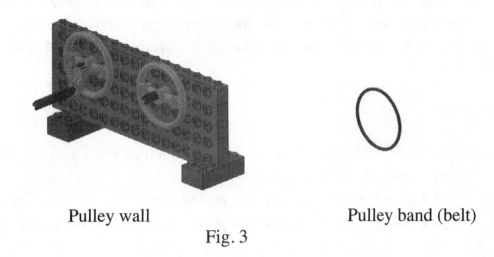

Pulley wall   Pulley band (belt)

Fig. 3

The teacher attaches a crank to one of the pulleys and describes this pulley as the driver pulley, the pulley that is starting or initiating the movement. He/she turns the crank and asks the students to observe the movement of the pulleys and the pulley belt. The pulleys that are moved by the driver pulley are called the follower pulleys.

The teacher explains the building project for the day: to build a sturdy pulley wall with at least four pulleys. The teacher explains that the team will first build a sturdy LEGO® wall. Then they will attach at least four pulleys to the wall. One of the pulleys will have a crank attached to it and this pulley will be the driver pulley. The team will use pulley belts to connect the pulleys. The teams should experiment with different pulley belts and different distances between the pulleys so that the pulley tension is correct and the pulley wall functions correctly. When the team turns the driver pulley all of the other pulleys should rotate.

The class is then divided into teams of two and the team begins building and testing their pulley walls. The teacher circulates among the teams problem solving and suggesting building ideas to them.

The class is assembled near the end of the period and the teams share their pulley walls. The teams should name their pulley wall and share some of the problems they encountered while building it. They should describe the strategies they used to solve their problems.

After sharing the pulley walls, the students should complete the Response Sheet: **Engineer's Journal.**

If possible, the pulley walls should be displayed for the school community to view. The pulley walls can then be disassembled at a convenient time. Students will be instructed on the care of LEGO® materials and to sort and store these materials.

Extensions:

- Experiment with other LEGO® pieces (such as hubs and bushings) to see which ones can serve as pulley wheels.
- Build a pulley wall where the last pulley goes faster than the driver?
- Build a pulley wall where the last pulley goes slower than the driver?

Assessment:

- Teacher's observations and interviews
- Building of a sturdy, pulley wall with at least 4 pulleys
- Completion of the Response Sheet: **Engineer's Journal**
- Completion of Response Sheet: **Assessment: Pulleys**

Sample Building Projects

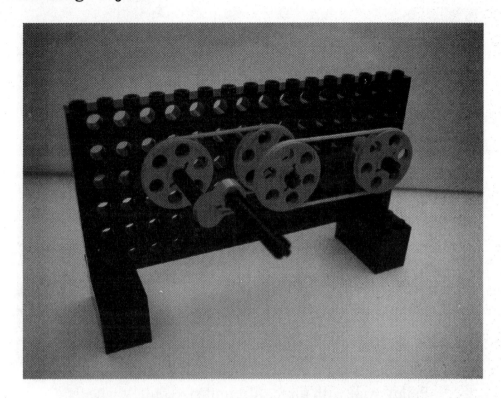

Pulley wall with all the same size pulley wheels

Pulley wall with one of the follower pulley wheels larger than the other pulleys

Pulley wall with three different size pulley wheels

Response Sheet:
Engineer's Journal

Engineer: _____ Date: _____

Teammate: _____

Name of Pulley Wall: _____

   1. Draw a picture of your pulley wall.

2. Write a sentence describing how you made the pulley wall.

_____

_____

_____

_____

_____

Response Sheet:
Assessment: Pulleys

Engineer: _____ Date: _____

1. Draw two pulleys. Color the pulleys blue. Connect them with a pulley belt. Color the belt red.

2. What happens if the pulley belt is **too loose**?

_____

_____

_____

3. What happens if the pulley belt is **too tight**?

_____

_____

_____

Grade One
Project Seven: Introduction to Motors

Project Objective: To investigate a 9-volt motor and experiment with its operation.

Time: One to two 45 minute periods

Materials:
- LEGO® Simple Machine or Mindstorm kits or other LEGO® pieces
- RCX or battery pack
- LEGO® 9-volt motor
- Internet/Literature: examples about machines with pictures of motors
- Batteries
- Scissors
- Tape
- Wire with LEGO® RCX terminals

Response Sheets:
- Engineer's Surprise
- Engineer Journal
- Assessment: Motors

Vocabulary:
- Motor
- Connecting wire with terminals
- Battery pack
- Batteries
- Primary colors

Procedure:

The teacher displays pictures or examples of motors found in his/her internet search and ask the students if anyone knows what the various examples are called and their uses. The teacher then identifies the objects, pointing out the location of the motor, and explains the uses made of motors.

The teacher then holds up a LEGO® motor for the class to observe (Fig. 1).

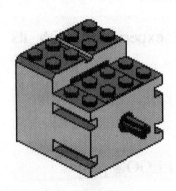

9 volt motor from
Mindstorm kit

9-volt motor from Simple
Machine kit

Fig. 1

He/she asks the students to make some observations about the motor, asking probing questions about motors such as:

- What is this LEGO® piece called?
- Where have you seen something like this?
- Do all motors look the same?
- Why were they invented?
- What does a motor do?
- What makes a motor run?
- Do all motors run on the same fuel?
- What does our LEGO® motor need to make it rotate?

The teacher then introduces the power the students will use to run the motor, which is either a battery pack or a RCX.

If you are using a battery pack, introduce the connecting wire, its two terminals and the battery pack (Fig. 2). Show the inside of the battery pack and count the batteries that are connected in series to provide the necessary voltage to operate the motor. Explain how the wires must make a metal to metal contact to send power to the motor. Demonstrate how the wire is connected to the battery pack. Draw attention to the metal contacts on all the terminals. Operate the motor. Also discuss the direction that the motor is rotating. Note that the direction of rotation can be changed by rotating the connecting wire on the battery pack by half a circle or 180°.

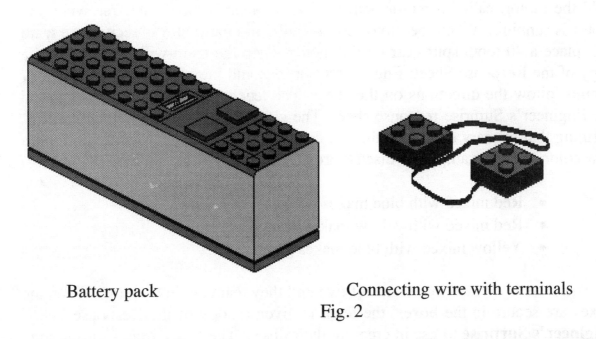

Battery pack   Connecting wire with terminals

Fig. 2

If you are using an RCX, introduce the connecting wire, its terminals and the RCX (Fig. 3). Show the battery compartment inside of the RCX and count the batteries that are connected in series to provide the necessary voltage to operate the motor. Explain how the wires must make a metal to metal contact to send power to the motor. Demonstrate how the wire is connected to the RCX. Demonstrate how to turn the RCX on and off. Draw attention to the metal contacts on all pieces. Operate the motor. Also discuss the direction that the motor is rotating and the direction of rotation can be changed by rotating the connecting wire on the RCX by half a circle or 180°.

The RCX   Connecting wire with terminals

Fig. 3

The teacher explains the building project: to build a LEGO® box that will hold the motor, called a motor box, so that the team's hands are free when the motor is running. When the motor box is built, and the motor is secure, the team will place a 40 tooth spur gear on the motor. Then the team will then be given a copy of the Response Sheet: Engineer's Surprise and they are reminded that they should follow the directions on the sheet. The teacher reviews the directions on the Engineer's Surprise response sheet. The class should discuss primary colors, defining that primary colors are those colors that can be mixed together to form a new color. Some examples to discuss are:

- Red mixed with blue makes purple
- Red mixed with yellow makes orange
- Yellow mixed with blue makes green.

The class is divided into teams of two and they team begin building. When the boxes are secure in the boxes, the team is given a copy of the Response Sheet: **Engineer's Surprise** to use in creating their discs. The teacher circulates among the teams problem solving and suggesting building ideas to the teams.

The class is assembled near the end of the period to share their motor boxes and their observations of the moving colors and patterns.

After discussing their findings, the students complete the Response Sheet: **Engineer's Journal.**

If possible, the motor boxes with colored discs should be displayed for the school community to view. They can then be disassembled at a convenient time. Students will be instructed on the care of LEGO® materials and to sort and store these materials.

The students complete the Response Sheet: **Assessment: Motors.**

Extensions:

- Design several different patterns for other discs, such as spirals, dots, arcs, circles and dashes.

Assessment:

- Teacher's observations and interviews
- Building of a sturdy, motor box.
- Demonstrate the correct use of motor to run it forward and reverse.
- Completion of the Response Sheet: Engineer's Journal
- Completion of the Response Sheet: Assessment: Motors

Sample Building Projects

Motor box with motor secured inside. The gear is ready for the colored disc to be
added. The RCX is ready to run the motor for the Engineer's Surprise.

Motor with box removed for viewing

Motor is secured by adding LEGO® pieces for support on the bottom, and sides.

Response Sheet:
Engineer's Journal

Engineer: _____ Date: _____

Teammate: _____

1. Draw a picture of your motor box. Also draw a picture of the colored disc.
   Color in the sections of the disc with the colors you used.

[Blank box for drawing]

2. Write a sentence describing what happened to the colors when the disc
   began to rotate.

   _____

   _____

   _____

3. What happens to the colors when you reversed the motor?

   _____

   _____

   _____

Response Sheet: Engineer's Surprise

Directions:
1. Color your circle with two primary colors that can be mixed together to make a new color.
2. Cut out the circles.
3. Push a 40 tooth spur gear on your motor.
4. Tape the colored circle to the motor.
5. Run the motor using the RCX or battery pack.
6. Observe the result.
7. Reverse the motor & observe the results.
8. Use the other circles to design your own paper disc.

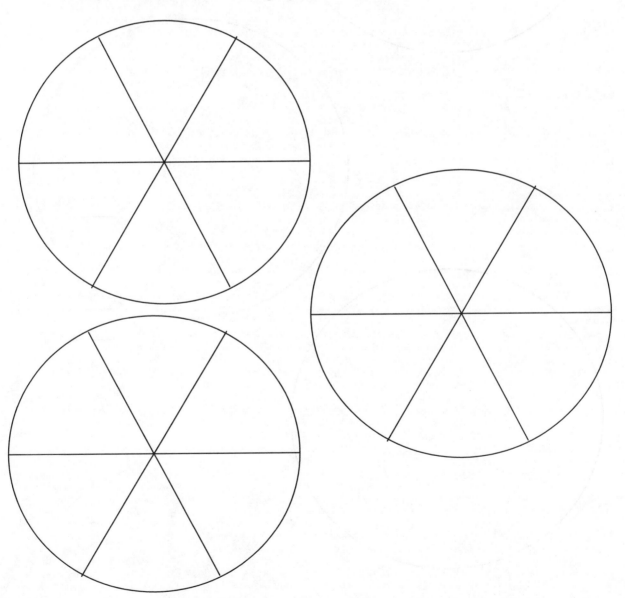

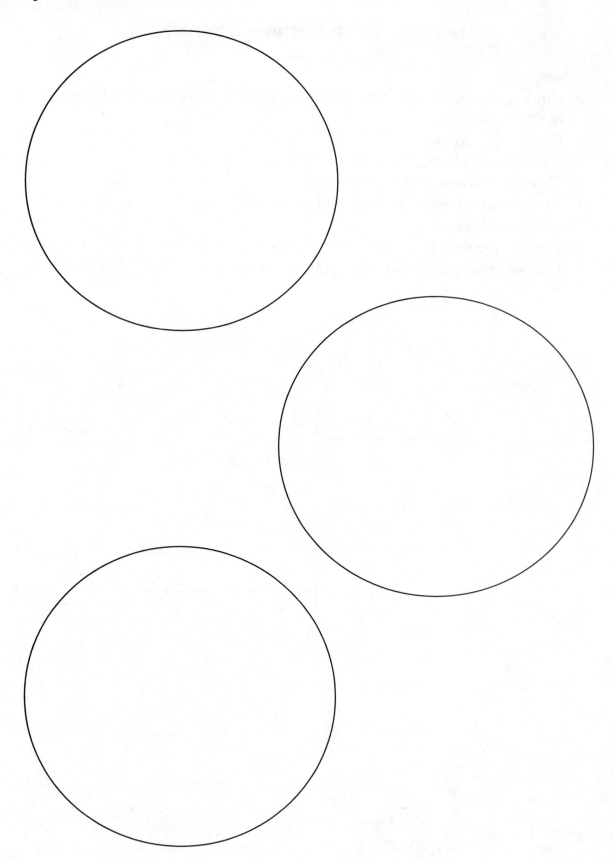

Response Sheet:
Assessment: Motors

Engineer: _____ Date: _____

1. Match the picture with its name by drawing a line to connect them.

Motor

Connecting Wire

Battery Pack

2. What happens if the connecting wire is **too loose** on its terminal?

_____

_____

3. How can you change the direction the motor is rotating?

_____

_____

Response Sheet:
Assessment: Motors

Engineer: _____ Date: _____

1. Match the picture with its name by drawing a line to connect them.

RCX

Connecting Wire

Motor

2. What happens if the connecting wire is **too loose** on the motor?

_____

_____

3. How can you change the direction the motor is rotating?

_____

_____

Grade One
Project Eight: Build a Car

Project Objective: To build and motorize a sturdy car using wheels and axles and a motor.

Time: Two to three 45 minute periods

Materials:
- LEGO® Simple Machine or Mindstorm kits
- Battery pack or RCX
- Batteries
- Teacher's Reference: Some Problems and Solutions

Response Sheet:
- Engineer's Journal

Vocabulary:
- Wheel
- Axle
- Chassis
- Friction
- Motor
- Connecting wire with terminals
- Battery pack or RCX
- Batteries
- Friction
- Sturdy

Procedure:

The teacher begins the project with a discussion about cars. He/she asks probing questions about cars such as:

- What does a car look like?
- How many wheels does it need?
- What will you have to do to make it move?
- What LEGO® pieces could you use to build it?

The teacher then introduces the topic for this project: to build a sturdy car that includes a motor. The motor will be attached to a battery pack or RCX, which will power it and make it roll. The teacher then asks the students to remember what LEGO® pieces are suitable for building the frame of the car, or the chassis such as axles, bushings and beams (Fig. 1).

Axle, bushing and beam
Fig. 1

He/she introduces the word chassis. The chassis is the frame of the car. As the class discusses the project and names the LEGO® parts needed to build the car, the teacher holds up that LEGO® piece and begins to demonstrate the procedure for building a simple car. The teacher shows the students how to insert the axles in the beams and to attach the bushings to support the axles. Next he/she indicates how to add the wheels to the axles (Fig. 2).

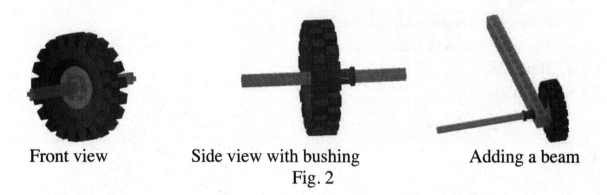

Front view   Side view with bushing   Adding a beam
Fig. 2

He/she reminds the students of the drop test from previous projects and demonstrates the drop test on his/her model. The class discusses some of the building strategies they remember for making structures sturdy.

The teacher asks the class how they will get the motor to turn the wheels (connect it to the axle). The teacher explains that the motor will be turning (rotating) one of the axles which will then rotate the wheels attached to that axle.

The other axle with its attached wheels will be rolled along (free wheeling) and will not need a motor to drive it. The teacher asks the students to think about other LEGO® projects they remember and to suggest a way to attach the motor to the axle (pulley system or meshed gears). The teacher then demonstrates how to attach the motor to the axle using a simple pulley system (Fig. 3). He/she then attaches the lead wire to the power source and operates the car.

Attaching pulley   Finished sample prototype

Fig. 3

The teacher introduces the word friction. Friction is a force that resists the movement of one object in contact with another. He/she should have the children rub their hands together and feel the heat. The heat generated is due to frictional forces.

The car has several places where friction might occur on their car and the teacher asks the class to predict where these places might be located (where the axle and the beam touch, where the wheels touch the floor, where the wheels touch the car). When the class suggests areas where friction occurs, the teacher demonstrates what happens to the car's motion with high friction by pushing the LEGO® pieces firmly together. He/she then adjusts the assembly to reduce or eliminate the cause of the friction. The teacher asks the class to suggest other ways to reduce the friction in these areas (loosen the connections, run on a tile floor rather than a rug).

The class is then divided into teams of two teammates to begin building and testing. The teacher circulates among the student teams problem solving and suggesting building ideas to them.

The class is assembled near the end of the period to discuss the design of their cars. Each team should identify a problem they encountered when building their car and what changes they made to solve that problem. After sharing their ideas, the students should complete the Response Sheet: **Engineer's Journal**.

If possible, the cars should be displayed for the school community to view. The cars should be saved to be used in Project Nine.

Extensions:

- Students can be given lights or other LEGO® pieces to mount on their car.
- Students to be a 'LEGO® Teacher' and share their skills with others.

Assessment:

- Teacher's observations and interviews
- Building of a sturdy, motorized car.
- Demonstrate the correct use of motor to run car forward and reverse.
- Completion of the Response Sheet: **Engineer's Journal**

Teacher's Reference:
Steps to build a sturdy car

Step one: Gather the materials for the basic frame.

The frame of a car includes the following LEGO® pieces (Parts List):

	Tire	Wheels are made from tires and hubs
	Hub	A hubs is the rigid center part of the wheel
	Bushing	Bushings keep things in place
	Axle	Wheels are attached (using the hubs) to an axle
	Beam	Beams form the structure of the car's chassis and provide the bearings to support the axles
	Plates	Plates form a base to which the motor is attached

Step Two: Build a frame or chassis for the car (Fig. 4).

Fig. 4: Partial car
        frame

Bushings, located on the shaft, are placed on each side of the beam to keep the tires from sliding back and forth. They should be close to the beam but not **too** close. If they are too close, the shaft will bind and not be able to turn freely. This binding/friction may prevent the car from moving.

Fig. 5 Sturdy car frame

It is important that the frame be as rectangular and symmetric as possible (Fig. 5). If the frame is crooked there will be more friction on one side than the other. The car will tend turn in the direction of the side with the highest friction force.

Step Three: Add a motor to the frame (Fig. 6).

Fig. 6 Adding a motor to the frame

Step Four: Boxing in the motor to support it (Fig. 7).

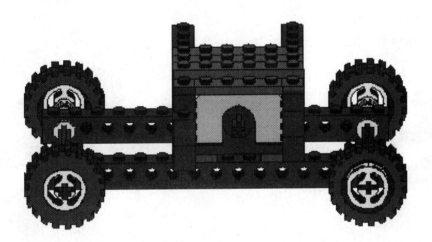

Fig. 7 Car with boxed-in motor

To prevent the car from coming apart when it is dropped from knee height, it is recommended that you box in the motor on all sides using plates and beams. The boxed in motor is supported in all directions and will not come apart easily.

Step Five: Connect the motor to the drive axle using a pulley system or meshed gears.

Step Six: Attach the terminal on one end of the connecting wire to the motor and the terminal on the other end to the battery pack or RCX.

Teacher's Reference
Some Problems and Solutions:

- Method for building a base to support the newer LEGO® motors making them flat. The solution to this problem is demonstrated below:

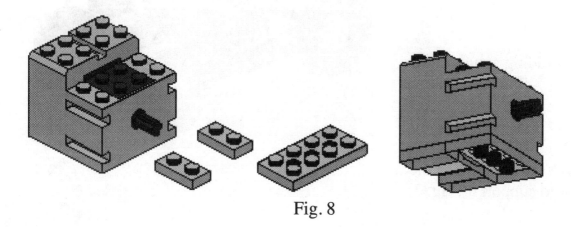

Fig. 8

Learning to 'box in' the motor anchoring it to the car's frame (Fig. 9)

Fig. 9

Learning to 'box in' the motor anchoring it to the car's frame (Fig. 10)

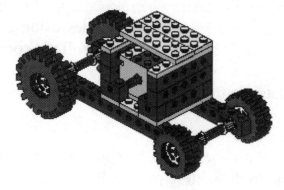

Fig. 10

Connecting the motor to the drive axle with a pulley (Fig. 11): Stretch the pulley band over the pulley of the motor and on the axle.

Fig. 11

Connecting the motor to the drive axle with gears (Fig. 12):

Fig. 12

Response Sheet
Engineer's Journal

Engineer: _____ Date: _____

Teammate: _____

1. Draw a picture of your car.

```




```

2. Write a sentence about a problem you encountered as you built your car.

_____

_____

_____

3. Write a sentence about how you solved a problem you encountered as you built your car.

_____

_____

_____

Grade One
Project Nine: Build a Snowplow

Project Objective: To use the engineering design process to design, build and test a prototype snowplow.

Time: Two to three 45 minute periods

Materials:
- LEGO® Simple Machine or Mindstorm kits
- Battery Pack or RCX
- Motorized cars from Project Eight
- Literature: *Katy and the Big Snow* by Virginia Lee Burton
- Internet search for pictures of snowplows
- Packing peanuts (as snow) and a roadway outlined on the floor with masking tape
- Poster of the Engineering Design Process (see background for teachers)
- Interactive whiteboard or easel mounted chart paper

Response Sheet:
- Engineer's Journal: Planning
- Engineer's Journal: Communications

Vocabulary:
- Plow
- Blade
- Engineer
- Prototype
- Motor
- Connecting wire and terminals
- Battery pack or RCX
- Friction
- Sturdy

Procedure:

The project begins with the teacher reading the book *Katy and the Big Snow* by Virginia Lee Burton or another snowplow related story. The class discusses the book, looking at the pictures of the snowplows. The teacher asks questions such as:

- What is the purpose of a snowplow?
- What shape is the blade on the snowplow?
- What direction does the plow face?
- Are the blades on every snowplow facing the same way?
- What other machines have a blade?
- Are the blades always the same?

The teacher displays the pictures of other snowplows that he/she found on the Internet and the class discusses features of the blade found on the snowplows.

The teacher displays the poster of the Engineering Design Process. He/she asks the students if anyone knows an engineer or what work an engineer performs. The class discusses engineering and creates a class definition for the word (a person who solves problems and makes our lives easier). The teacher records the definition on the interactive whiteboard or the chart paper. He/she explains that when engineers solve problems they go through a process to help them arrive at the best possible solution. The teacher then goes through the Engineering Design Process illustrated on the poster, describing each step. When Step Five is described, the teacher describes what a prototype is and the class creates a class definition for the word. The definition is written on the interactive whiteboard or the chart paper.

The teacher explains the engineering challenge: to design, build and test a prototype snowplow that can push a pile of "snow" (packing peanuts) off a roadway. He/she explains that the team will be adding a blade to their cars from the previous project and redesigning the car to be a snowplow. When the teams design the plow, they need to consider the direction of the blade and where they want the snow to go. They also need to think about how they will attach the blade to their cars. He/she explains that they will be working on Steps Three through Eight in the Engineering Design Process. They will begin with Step

Three, developing possible solutions. The teacher explains that when the teams are ready to test their prototypes, they will test their design on a roadway with packing peanuts to represent snow. The teacher displays the roadway and explains how to use it.

The teacher gives each student a copy of the Response Sheet: **Engineer's Journal: Planning**. The students are grouped into their teams from the last project and instructed to work together to complete the planning stage by completing this Response Sheet. The teacher goes over the sheet with the students. The teams are instructed to discuss their ideas together and draw a snowplow that they might build using the LEGO® building pieces and the car from the previous project. The teams should check with the teacher to obtain his/her approval before they begin to build their prototype. They will then work on Steps Four through Eight of the Engineering Design Process, building, testing and redesigning their prototype.

The class re-assembles near the end of the project. The teacher reviews the class definitions for an engineer and a prototype. He/she asks the teams to report on their progress in working like an engineer when they designed, built, and tested their prototype. Each team introduces their plow, shows how they attached the blade of the plow, and demonstrates how it works when it plows the snow. The team identifies a problem they encountered when building the plow or a modification they made to their original design they planned to build. The team shares what they did to solve that problem or why they needed to modify their plan.

After sharing, the students should complete the Response Sheet: **Engineer's Journal: Communication.**

If possible, the snowplows should be displayed for the school community to view. They can then be disassembled at a convenient time. Students will be instructed on the care of LEGO® materials and on how to sort and store these materials.

Extensions:

- Teams can add a cabin for the snowplow driver.
- If teams used pulleys and belts in their design, they can change the drive using meshed gears.
- Encourage students to be a 'LEGO® Teacher' and share their skills with others.

Assessment:

- Teacher's observations and interviews
- Building of a sturdy, motorized snowplow which can push the snow peanuts.
- Completion of the Response Sheet: Engineer's Journal: Planning
- Completion of Response Sheet: Engineer's Journal:: Communicate

Sample Building Projects

Blade added to the front by extending the car frame

Blade attached to the car using two friction pins

Blade variation using lever arms

Background for Teachers
Steps of the Engineering Design Process

From: *Massachusetts Science and Technology/Engineering Curriculum Framework, October 2006*

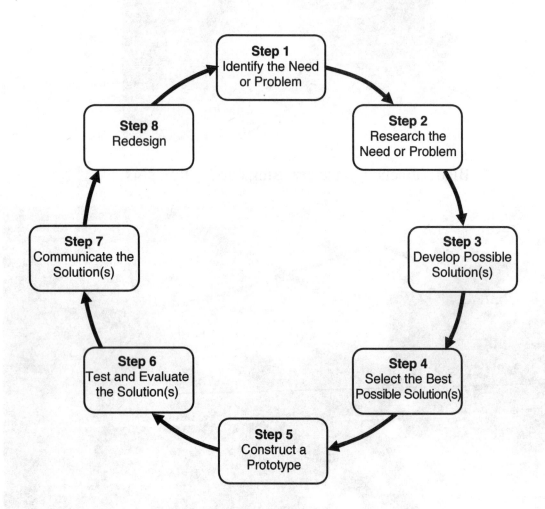

Steps in the Process Include:

1. Identify the need or problem
2. Research the need or problem
    - Examine the current state of the issue and current solutions
    - Explore other options via the Internet, library, interviews, etc.
3. Develop possible solution(s)
    - Brainstorm possible solution(s)
    - Draw on mathematics and science knowledge
    - Articulate the possible solution(s) in two and three dimensions
    - Refine the possible solution(s)
4. Select the best possible solution(s)
    - Determine which solution(s) best meet(s) the original need or solve(s) the original problem
5. Construct a prototype
    - Model the selected solution(s) in two and three dimensions
6. Test and evaluate the solution(s)
    - Does it work?
    - Does it meet the original design constraints?
7. Communicate the solution(s)
    - Make an engineering presentation that includes a discussion of how the solution(s) best meet(s) the initial need or the problem
    - Discuss societal impact and tradeoffs of the solution(s)
8. Redesign
    - Overhaul the solution(s) based on information gathered during the tests and presentation

Response Sheet
Engineer's Journal: Planning

Engineer: _____ Date: _____

Teammate: _____

1. Draw a picture of the snowplow you are thinking of building.

2. Draw a picture of your plan for attaching the plow to your car.

Response Sheet
Engineer's Journal: Communicate

Engineer: _____ Date: _____

Teammate: _____

1. Draw a picture of the snowplow you built.

2. Compare this picture to the picture you drew when you were planning. Write a sentence about how the prototype you built **differs** from what you were planning to build.

_____

_____

_____

3. Write a sentence about a problem you encountered as you were building the prototype and what changes you made to solve that problem.

_____

_____

_____

Teacher's Reference:

To build a stiff frame, use two narrow plates and two wider plates as illustrated below:

Building stiff LEGO® structures.

The LEGO kits contain many different types of pins and bushings to aid you in constructing interesting structures. Several connector pins and bushings are illustrated below:

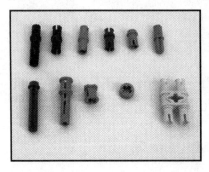

LEGO connector pins and bushings.

The illustrations on this page are from Eric Wang's book titled Engineering with LEGO® Bricks and Robolab, 2nd edition. The author thanks Eric for permission to use the photographs and the captions.

Grade

Two

Grade Two
Project One: Introduction to LEGO Building

Project Note: This set of building projects in Grade Two explores several different simple machines: wheel and axle; gears; pulleys and levers. The projects pair well with a read-aloud, book organized in chapters, and can be integrated into a literature unit. Charlotte's Web by E. B. White is a good reference for the building experiences gained in these projects.

Project Objective: To familiarize students with LEGO® vocabulary and specific building pieces.

Time: One to two 45 minute periods.

Materials:
- LEGO® Mindstorm or Simple Machine kits or other LEGO® building pieces
- Handout: Engineer Checklist
- Tray

Response Sheet:
- Recording My Science Observations

Vocabulary:
- LEGO® bricks
- LEGO® beams
- LEGO® separator

Procedure:

The project begins with a teacher led discussion about engineering and LEGO® blocks. The teacher may ask questions such as:

- Do you know anyone who is an engineer?
- What do you think an engineer does?
- Who has built with LEGO® blocks before?
- What structures have you made?

Then, the students are presented with their first LEGO® challenge which is to gather specific LEGO® pieces and, with a teammate, build a structure using just those pieces collected. The class is divided into teams of two and each student receives a checklist. The teacher previews the checklist with the students, holding up each LEGO® piece for the students to see and reviewing the name of the piece. The students are then instructed, as a team, to use their checklist to find specified pieces from the classroom bins or the Mindstorm or Simple Machines LEGO® kits to build with (Fig. 1). The teacher circulates around the room, answering questions and suggesting building ideas to the teams. As teams finish building, the students complete the Response Sheet: Recording My Science Observations.

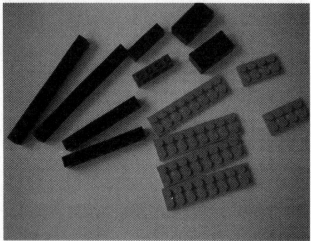

Fig. 1

Next, the teacher encourages the student teams to share their structure with another team of students. Following the sharing, the teacher leads the students in a discussion where they respond to the following questions:

- Where do you see bricks, plates and beams being used in your homes or school?
- How are the LEGO® pieces similar or different?
- How are the pieces organized?

The last question should lead into the final part of the project. Students will be instructed on how to properly care for, and put away the LEGO® materials.

Extensions:
- Have the student teams build the flattest or highest possible structure with the allotted pieces
- Pairs of student teams can connect their structures to create a new structure.

Assessment:

- Completion the Engineer's Checklist
- Completion of Response Sheet: Recording My Science Observations
- Naming various pieces such as bricks, beams, or plates
- Sorting pieces into their assigned bins
- Teacher observations and interviews

Sample Building Projects

A LEGO bed

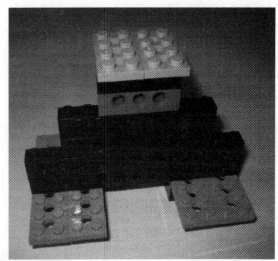

A LEGO wall

A LEGO alien

Teacher's Reference

Fig. 1 LEGO® spacing: 2 Units (left),
4 Units (middle), and 6 Units (right).
Count the spaces between the holes

Fig. 2 Building stiff LEGO® structures by using
two wide plates on opposite sides of the frame.

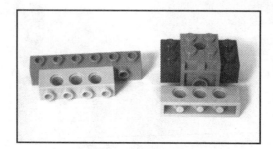

Fig. 3 Two methods for building right angles. On the right a right angle plate is
employed. On the left a few light gray ½ pins were inserted into the holes of the
1 × 6 beam. This arrangement works because the stud end of the ½ pin has the
same dimensions as the studs found on the top of a standard brick.

Fig. 4 The light gray ½ pin.

The four photographs on this page are by the courtesy of Eric Wang.

Engineer's Checklist

Engineer: _____ Date: _____

Teammate: _____

1. Collect the following LEGO® pieces and place them on your tray.

____ Two 2 × 4 bricks   ____ Two 1 × 4 beams

____ Two 1 × 8 beams   ____ Four 2 × 4 plates

____ Four 2 × 8 plates

____ Two 1 × 12 beams

____ One separator

2. Build a structure with your teammates using the pieces on your checklist. The separator can be used to take LEGO® pieces apart.

Response Sheet

Recording My Science Observations

Name: _____ Date: _____

Today, with my team, I built a simple structure out of specific LEGO® pieces.

My picture of what I built:

My observations:

_____

_____

_____

_____

_____

Grade Two
Project Two: Wheel and Axle

Project Objective: To build a tractor from Wilbur's barn that holds a miniature farm animal. This project assumes you are reading the book Charlotte's Web to the students. Modify the discussion if you are not using the book.

Time: One to two 45 minute periods.

Materials:
- Pictures of farm machinery
- LEGO® Mindstorm or Simple Machine kits or LEGO® building pieces
- Miniature farm animal or stuffy animal (children bring from home)
- Book- Charlotte's Web by E. B. White

Response Sheet:
- Building Design Sheet: A Tractor

Vocabulary:
- Tractor

Procedure:

Prior to initiating the project, acquire pictures of farm machinery to share with the class. Also instruct the students to bring in to class a small farm animal or stuffed animal from home to use in their building project. The project begins with a short discussion about Charlotte's Web and the barnyard. Direct the discussion to include the kinds of farm machines that might be stored in the barn. Questions you might ask could include:

- What are some of the farm machines you remember from a visit to a farm?
- Why does the farmer need to use these machines?

The teacher then explains to the students that they will be designing and building a tractor similar to one that might be found in Wilbur's barn. The tractor must hold the miniature farm animal or stuffy animal that they brought from home. The teacher asks the children if they remember how to build a sturdy car from their experiences in the previous year. He /she reviews the key components of a sturdy car. The teacher explains that the teams will not be mounting a motor and pulley on their tractor today, but that they will power their car (tractor) at another time later in the year.

The class is divided into teams of two and each student receives the student work sheet, **Building Design Sheet: A Tractor**. The teacher explains to the class that they will first draw and write about their tractor design individually. They will build it large enough to hold their small farm animal or stuffy comfortably. When the sheet is completed the teammates will talk about their ideas with each other. The teams should discus ways to use both of their ideas from the design sheet in their tractor. When they agree on the design, the teammates will build the tractor together.

The class assembles at the end of the period to share their tractors with the stuffy sitting in it. The teams should discuss some of the problems they encountered and the strategies they used to solve these problems. If possible, the teacher should call attention to the way the tractors are constructed or ways they are unusual.

If possible, the tractors should be displayed for the school community to view until they are needed in Project Six.

Extensions:

- Modify the tractor to tow a sled or trailer.
- Modify the tractor cab to provide shade for the miniature farm animal

Assessment:

- Completion of Building Design Sheet: A Tractor
- Completion of the challenge with teacher interview and observations

Sample Building Projects

A LEGO® tractor

A LEGO® pulley wheel and axle pin arranged to become a steering wheel.

Building Design Sheet: A Tractor

Engineer: _____ Date: _____

Teammate: _____

Challenge: To build a tractor from Wilbur's barn that can hold a miniature farm animal.

1. Draw your idea:

2. Describe your idea in writing:

_____

_____

_____

_____

3. Now share your plans with a partner.

Grade Two
Project Three: Gears

Project Objective: To familiarize students with gears and to design and build a simple gear system.

Time: Three to four 45 minute periods

Materials:
- LEGO®Mindstorm or Simple Machine kits or LEGO® building pieces Including different size gears, pointers and cranks.
- Pictures of gears found in everyday items.
- Examples of products with gears (such as a hand held egg beater, salad spinner, can opener, bicycle)

Response sheets:
- Exploring Gears
- Gearing Up and Gearing Down
- Gear Assessment

Vocabulary:
- Spur Gear
- Follower
- Driver
- Mesh
- Crank
- Tooth/teeth
- Pointer
- Clockwise
- Counterclockwise
- Rotate/rotation

Procedure:

The project begins with a teacher lead discussion about gears. The teacher should display different pictures of gears in everyday things, such as egg beaters, bicycles, and can openers. The teacher may ask questions such as:

- Why do people use gears?
- How do gears work?
- Why do you think you would use gears in building something?

Next, the teacher shows the students a diagram of a gear system (See Fig. 1) with the vocabulary words: gear, tooth/teeth, driver, follower, axle, crank and pointer.

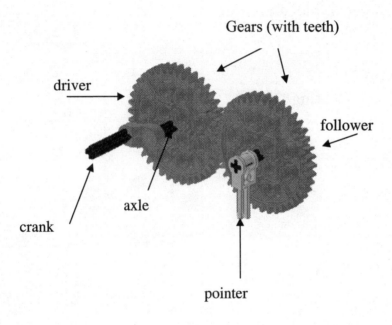

Fig. 1

The teacher introduces the words and shows where they are in the diagram (Fig. 1). He/she explains what they do. A gear is a wheel with teeth. These gears are called spur gears. The axle holds the gear and turns it when the crank is turned. The pointer turns as the gear turns, allowing us to see and count the movement of the gear more easily. The teacher introduces the word mesh when he/she meshes the two spur gears together. He/she explains that when the teeth of one gear touch the teeth of another gear, it is called meshing of the gears. Meshed gears turn each other.

Next the teacher assembles a model of a gear drive using LEGO® building pieces, naming each piece as he/she adds it to the model. (See Fig. 2)

Fig. 2

When he/she adds the gears, the word tooth is introduced and the number of teeth on that gear is counted. The teacher does the same thing with the driver and follower gears. A crank is added to the driver gear and this word is introduced to the students. The teacher asks the students. "If I turn this crank one turn, what do you predict the follower will do?" The teacher accepts all predictions and says "Let's try it." The teacher turns the driver one turn and asks, **"What happened?"** (the follower turns). The teacher adds a pointer to the follower gear and introduces the new piece. He/she explains that the pointer will help them count the number of turns, or rotations, made by the follower gear. The teacher defines the words rotate and rotation. The teacher turns the driver and has the students watch the pointer turns on the follower gear.

The teacher then introduces the project. He/she explains that the students will be working in teams of two. The team will be designing, building and exploring the gears together, completing the Response Sheets as they work. Give each student the Response Sheet: **Exploring Gears**.

Review the Response Sheet, answering questions that the students might have. The teams then begin the project, following the directions on the response sheet. As the teams finish **Exploring Gears,** the teacher reviews their responses for accuracy and completeness. The teacher then gives them the second Response Sheet: **Gearing Up and Gearing Down** and asks them to complete it.

After completing both Response Sheets, the teacher leads the students in a concluding discussion about the project with questions such as:

- What is something new that you learned about gears?
- Have you seen any gears like those in the models you built?
- What was your power source for turning the gears?
- How did you get the follower to move the same direction as the driver? Move in the opposite directions than the driver?
- What did you do to get the follower to move faster than the driver? Move slower than the driver?

Students are instructed on how to properly care for, and put away the LEGO® materials. The **Gear Assessment** Sheet should be given at the end of the project.

Extensions:

- When the teams complete these activities, they can be given additional gears to expand their structures and gear drives and explore the results.
- When the teams complete these activities, they can be given crown gears to examine.

Assessment:

- Successful completion of the Response Sheets: Exploring Gears and Gearing Up and Gearing Down
- Completion of Gear Assessment Sheet

Response Sheet
Exploring Gears

Engineer: _____ Date: _____

Teammate: _____

Use the list below to obtain the materials needed for this project.
Parts List:

Name of part	Number needed	picture
1x 16 beam	2	
2x 4 brick	4	
40-tooth gear	2	
Crank	1	
Pointer	1	
6 stud axle	2	
3 stud axle	1	
Bushing	2	

Response Sheet
Exploring Gears

Engineer: _____ Date: _____

Teammate: _____

1. Build a gear model that looks like this.
   You will need a Parts List:

Name of Lego building piece	Number needed
24-tooth spur gear	2
6-stud axle	2
4- stud axle	1
1 x 16 beam	2
2 x 4 brick	4
Crank	1
Pointer	1

2. On this picture, label the driver, follower, crank, and pointer.

3. How many **teeth** are on each gear? Count them and write the number in the space provided. Driver _____ Follower _____

4. Predict what will happen when you turn the driver clockwise:

   _____

   _____

5. Try it. Write down what you observed.

   _____

   _____

6. Complete the chart for this model:

Number of turns of the driver	**Predict** the number of turns of the follower	**Observed the** number of turns of the follower
2		
5		
10		

7. Now change your model to look like this.

The extra pieces you will need are:

Name of Lego building piece	Number needed
8-tooth spur gear	1
6-stud axle	1
Bushing	1

8. The middle gear is called an **idler**. How many **teeth** does this idler have?

_____

9. Predict what will happen to the **idler** gear and **follower** gear when you turn the **driver** gear clockwise:

_____

_____

10. Try it, and write what you observed.

_____

_____

11. What was the job of the **idler** gear?

_____

_____

12. Which gear moved **fastest**? (check only one)

    □ driver   □ idler   □ follower

Why do you believe this gear moved the fastest?

_____

_____

Reflect on what you have learned about gears and how they moved in this project. Describe in writing three things you learned.

   1._____

_____

   2._____

_____

   3. _____

_____

Response Sheet
Gearing Up

Engineer: _____ Date: _____

Teammate: _____

Examine this model. Then complete the chart below, listing the number of pieces you will need to collect of each LEGO® part.

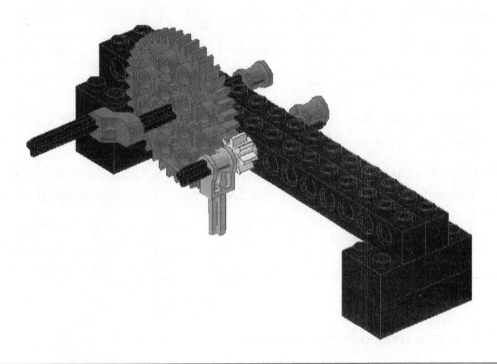

Part Name	Number Required
1 × 16 beam	
2 × 4 brick	
40-tooth gear	
8-tooth gear	
Bushing	
6 stud axle	
3 stud axle	
Pointer	
Crank	

Gather the parts you require using your parts list. Then build the model. Answer the following questions about your model.

1. How many teeth are on the follower gear? _____

2. Predict what will happen when you turn the driver clockwise:

_____

_____

3. turn the driver clockwise. Describe in writing what you observed.

_____

_____

4. Complete the chart for this gear train:

Number of turns of the driver	**Predict** the number of turns of the follower	**Observe the** number of turns of the follower
1		
2		
5		

5. Which gear rotated fastest? (check one)

☐ driver   ☐ follower

6. Why do you think this gear rotates faster?

_____

_____

7. When the follower rotates faster than the driver, it is called **gearing up**. Can you think of a time when you might want the follower to rotate faster than the driver?

_____

_____

Response Sheet
Gearing Down

Engineer: _____ Date: _____

Teammate: _____

Now change your model to look like the one shown below:

1. What is different about this model compared to the one you examined before?

   _____

   _____

2. How many teeth are on the driver gear? ____ How many teeth are on the follower gear? _____

3. Predict what will happen to the follower gear when you turn the driver gear clockwise:

   _____

   _____

4. Turn the driver gear clockwise and describe your observation in writing.

_____

_____

5. Complete the chart for this gear train:

Number of turns of the driver	**Predict** the number of turns of the follower	**Observe the** number of turns of the follower
1		
5		
10		

6. Which gear rotated slowest? (check one)

  ☐ driver   ☐ follower

7. Why do you think this gear rotated slower than the other gear?

_____

_____

8. When the follower rotates more slowly than the driver, it is called **gearing down**. Can you think of a time when you might want the follower to rotate slower than the driver?

_____

_____

9. Draw a picture of two meshed gears that are **geared up**. Write a fact about these gears in the box provided below.

10. Draw a picture of two meshed gears that are **geared down**. Write a fact about these gears in the box provided below.

Response Sheet:
Gear Assessment

Engineer: _____ **Date:** _____

1. Design and build a gear train in which the driver and the follower turn at the same speed, but in opposite directions. Prepare a drawing of what you designed and built.

2. Design and build a gear train in which the driver and the follower turn at the same speed, but in the same directions. Prepare a drawing of what you designed and built.

3. Design and build a gear train in which the driver turns 5 times faster than the follower. Prepare a drawing of what you designed and built.

Grade Two
Project Four: Crown Gears

Project Objective: To build a rotating sign for Wilber's farm using a crown gear together with other gears.

Time: Three to four 45 minute periods

Materials:
- LEGO® Mindstorm or Simple Machine kits or LEGO® building pieces, including crown gears
- Hand egg beater
- Hand made sign for the farm
- Book- Charlotte's Web by E. B. White
- Building Design Sheet: A Sign for the Farm
- Paper & Crayons/Markers for sign making

Response Sheet:
- Reflection: A Sign for the Farm
- Crown Gear Assessment

Vocabulary:
- Crown gear
- Rotate/Rotation
- Mesh

Procedure:

The project begins with a review of what was learned about gears in the last project. The teacher reviews the names and parts of the gear system that the students constructed in the last project. In the review, include probing questions such as:

- Where have you seen gears?
- What are their uses?
- What did the driver gear do?
- What did the follower gear do?
- Does anyone remember what they did to increase the speed of the follower gear? (Geared up)

- What was this arrangement was called?
- Does anyone remember how they decreased the speed of the follower gear? (Geared down)
- Where might you find a gear drive that has been geared up? (egg beater, salad spinner)
- Where might you find a gear drive that has been geared down? (bicycle)

The teacher holds up a crown gear and asks if anyone has seen this type of gear before and if they know what it is called. He/she introduces the crown gear by holding it next to a spur gear from the last project and asks the students to make some observations about the two gear's differences and the similarities (Fig. 1).

24 tooth crown gear   24 tooth spur gear

Fig. 1

The teacher asks the students if they can think of uses for the crown gear. The teacher explains that crown gears are use to change the orientation of the axle, such as from horizontal to vertical or from east to west. He/she holds up a hand egg beater and turns the handle (crank) and asks the students to observe what the egg beater is doing (Fig. 2). The teacher explains that the crown gear on the egg beater changes the orientation of the axle driving the rotating beaters, making it easier to beat eggs. He/she introduces the word rotate.

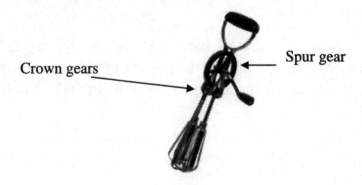

Crown gears   Spur gear

Fig. 2

The teacher then introduces the project. He/she explains that the students will be working in design teams of two. The team will be designing, building and testing a sign that rotates or turns. The sign will advertise Wilber's farm. The sign must be rotated with a crank and the design must use a crown gear. The team must first describe their design with a drawing and a written description before they start building.

The teacher assigns the teams and gives each student the **Design Sheet: A Sign for the Farm**. The teacher reviews the design sheet with the students and explains that the sheet must be completed by the team before any building begins. He/she explains that the when the team complete the design sheet, they should check in with the teacher for your approval before they begin building.

When work on the rotating signs is complete, assemble the class to share their ideas and display their structures. Ask each team to show how their structure functions and to share their pride over one of their special ideas. Then ask each team to share some problem they encountered when they were building and to describe their solution for that problem. As a conclusion to the project, ask each student to complete the **Response Sheet Reflection: A Sign for the Farm**.

If possible, the rotating signs should be displayed for the school community to view. The rotating signs should **be saved** to be used with the next project on worm gears.

Students should complete the **Response sheet: Crown Gear Assessment**.

Extensions:

- Change the gearing of the gears to make the sign rotate faster/slower

Assessment:

- Student Design Sheet: A Sign for the Farm
- Completion of the challenge with teacher interview and observations
- Completion of the Response Sheet: Reflection: A Sign for Wilber's Farm
- Completion of the Response Sheet: Crown Gear Assessment

Project examples:

Sample meshed crown gear and 24 tooth spur gear

Team Project example

Parts list for an example and assembly directions for a Crown Gear Drive:

Gather all the following pieces

- Four 1 × 12 beams

- Four 2 × 4 bricks

- One 2 × 4 plate, no holes

- One 2 × 8 plate, with holes

- One 24 tooth crown gear

- One 24 tooth spur gear

- Two bushings

- One crank

- One #4 axle

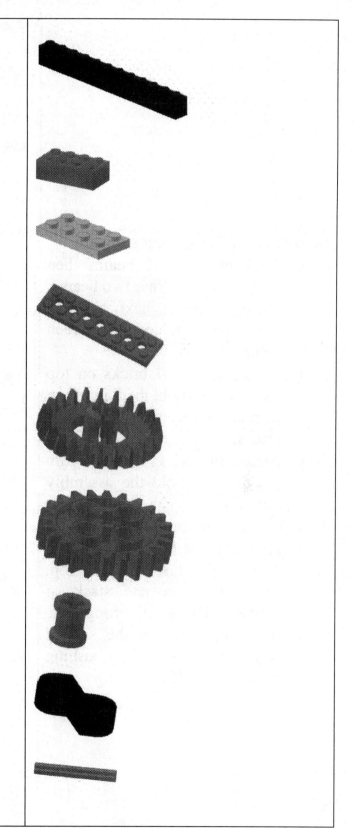

• One #8 axle	
• One #12 axle	

Step 1: Assemble support structure
- Stack two 1 × 12 beams then repeat with the other two beams. Stand them up next to each other with a space between them.
- Stack two 2 × 4 bricks on top the beams to hold them in place. Repeat with the other two bricks.
- Attach the bricks to the beam assembly to hold the assembly securely.

Step 2: Assemble and attach gear
- Attach the 24 tooth spur gear to the #8 axle. Insert it into a top, center hole on one stack of beams. Thread it through the other top hole on the second stack of beams. Add a bushing to hold the axle in place.

Step 3: Attach the crank
- Attach the crank to the axle.
- Insert the # 4 axle in the other end of the crank.

Step 4: Install the plate
- Attach the 2 × 4 plate to the beam assembly.

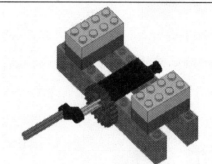

Step 5: Assemble and attach the crown gear
- Attach the 24 tooth crown gear to the #12 axle. Place a bushing on the axel to secure the gear.
- Insert the axle and gear in the hole on the 2 × 4 plate, so that the crown gear's teeth mesh with the spur gear's teeth. .

Step 6: Install the top plate
- Attach the 2 × 8 plate to the brick assembly to hold the #12 axle in place.
- Create a sign and attach it to the axle.

Design Sheet:
A Sign for the Farm

Engineer: _____ Date: _____

Teammate: _____

1. Prepare a drawing of the design you are considering building:

2. Color the crown gear **red**.

3. Describe your design in writing.

_____

_____

_____

_____

_____

Response Sheet
Reflection: A Sign for the Farm

Engineer: _____ Date: _____

Teammate: _____

    1. Prepare a drawing of what you built:

    2. Color the crown gear **red**.

    3. Look at the picture you drew at the start of this project. Reflect on how it is different from what you built. Describe some of your thoughts in writing.

_____

_____

_____

    4. Reflect on your building. Why did you build your rotating sign differently from what you originally thought you would build?

_____

_____

_____

Response Sheet:
Crown Gear Assessment

Engineer: _____ **Date:** _____

1. Examine Figure 1.

Draw an arrow from the vocabulary word in the box to its picture in Figure 1.

| Spur gear | | Crown gear |

Fig. 1

2. Describe how you know when two gears are meshed.

_____

_____

_____

_____

Grade Two
Project Five: Worm Gears

Project Objective: To slow down the speed of the rotating sign for Wilber's farm by using a worm gear.

Time: Three to four 45 minute periods

Materials:
- LEGO® Mindstorm or Simple Machine kits
- Worm gear in gear box
- RCX or Battery Pack
- Wire with LEGO® RCX terminals
- Rotating signs from Project Four
- Design Sheet: Motorizing the Sign
- Book: Mindstorms for Schools Using ROBOLAB (A resource for the extensions of this project)
- Interactive whiteboard or easel mounted chart paper

Response Sheet:
- The Worm Gear
- Reflection: A Motorized Sign for the Farm

Vocabulary:
- Worm gear
- Gear down
- RCX

Procedure:

The lesson begins with a review of what was learned about gears during the last project. The teacher displays some of the rotating signs retained from the last project and reviews how the crown gear was useful in changing the orientation of the axle about which the sign rotated.

The teacher asks how the students might motorize the sign so that they do not have to turn it by hand. Expect an answer that says something like "just attach the motor". **As a demonstration only**, the teacher should remove the crank and just attach a motor to the axle, attach the wire with LEGO® RCX terminals to the motor and to the RCX/battery pack (Caution: signs will rotate quickly. Do not allow students to do this.)

The teacher then runs the RCX so the student can observe the moving sign. The sign will turn very rapidly and be difficult to read. The teacher asks the students to make some observations about the sign and how fast it is rotating. He/she asks the students to think about how they might slow down the moving sign so people can read it. On the interactive whiteboard or the chart paper create a list of the ideas the students suggest and discuss the different solutions. The students will probably suggest some of the ideas that would work to slow down the sign such as programming the motor in ROBOLAB to turn more slowly or to gear down the sign.

The teacher then tells the class that he/she will be introducing another type of gear that works well to slow things down. He/she holds up a worm gear box assembly (Fig. 1) and begins to take it apart, introducing the parts that make up the whole.

Worm Gear Box
Fig. 1

The teacher should display the pictures of the parts of the assembly on chart paper, writing the part name underneath the part's picture (see **Example: Worm Gear Assembly**).

The teacher explains that the students will be working on the same team as the last lesson, using the rotating signs saved from that lesson. The teams will be learning about worm gears and how they work by building worm gear assemblies like the one the teacher just showed to the class. The teacher gives each student a copy of **Response Sheet: The Worm Gear** and reviews the sheet with the students.

The teacher has the teams build the worm gears, completing the response sheets. Allow 10-15 minutes for this part of the project. When the class has finished the response sheet, have the group come back in large group discussion and go over the answers the teams recorded. The teacher asks the teams to report on how many times they turned the worm to move the 24-tooth spur gear one time. The teacher then demonstrates to the class how to determine the correct answer by turning the pointer on the worm gear and having the students count aloud the number of rotations. The pointer on the worm gear should turn 24 times before the pointer on the spur gear returns to its original position. The worm gear will slow down the spur gear, and anything attached to it, by 24 times (Fig. 2).

Step 2: Watch this pointer move, stop turning (in step 1) when this pointer returns to the original position.

Step 1: Turn this pointer, counting the number of times you turn it one full (360°) turn.

Fig. 2

The teacher asks the class to think about the original problem they had with their signs, which they turned too fast. He/she asks the students to think about how they might use the worm gear to slow down their signs. The class discusses how to attach the worm gear to the original sign and how to attach a motor to the worm gear. The teacher introduces an axle joiner, a LEGO® part used to connect two axles (Fig. 3).

Axle joiner (coupling).
Fig. 3

The teacher then explains that the teams must first prepare a drawing of their design and then write a description of their design before starting to build their gear drives. The teacher gives each student a copy of the Design Sheet: **Motorizing the Sign**. He/she goes over the sheet with the students and reminds each team that the teacher must approve the design before they begin building it.

When the teams have completed their gear drives they should check with the teacher to obtain your approval before they are given an RCX to use. LEGO® motors are attached to Port A using connector wires. The motors will operate when connected to this port without additional programming.

When the motorized rotating signs are completed, assemble the class to share their ideas and to display their structures. Ask each team to describe how they attached the motors and to share a problem they encountered during the design and building process. The students should describe their solution to this problem.

As a conclusion to the project, ask each student to complete the Response Sheet: **Reflection: A Motorized Sign for the Farm.**

If possible, the motorized rotating signs should be displayed for the school community to view. They can then be disassembled at a convenient time. Students will be instructed on the care of LEGO® materials and to sort and store these materials.

Extensions:

- Use ROBOLAB to program the sign to turn one direction for 4 seconds and stop.
- Use ROBOLAB to program the sign to turn one direction for 6 seconds and then reverse direction for 6 seconds before stopping.
- Use ROBOLAB to add music to the program rotating the sign.

Programming the RCX for the Extensions

- Students should open the Programmer section of ROBOLAB on a computer (Fig. 4).

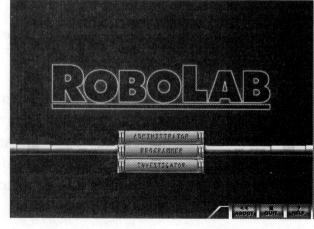

Fig. 4

- Select Pilot 1 for a single step program. Students should select the time (clock) icon by clicking and dragging the clock with the mouse. They can then select the 4-seconds icon. They then click the large white arrow to download the program on their RCX through the IR tower (Fig. 5).

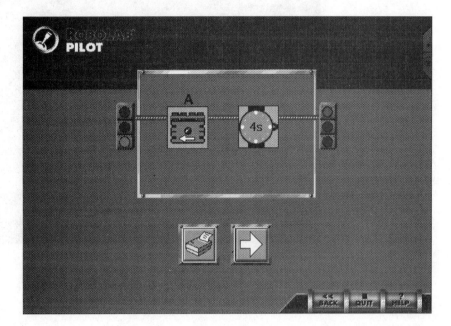

Fig. 5

- Select Pilot 3 for a two step program to control the direction of the rotation of the sign first in one direction and then the other (Fig. 6).

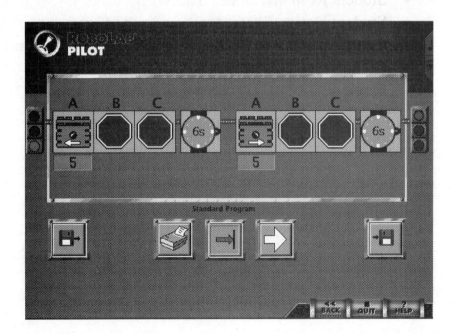

Fig. 6

- Music can be added to all programs by selecting the music icon in the upper right hand corner of the Robolab Pilot screen (Fig. 7).

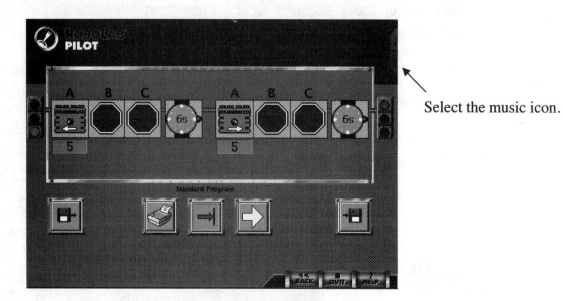

Select the music icon.

Fig. 7

Assessment:

- Student Response Sheet: The Worm Gear
- Student Design Sheet: Motorizing the Sign
- Completing the challenge with teacher interview and observations.
- Completing the Response Sheet Reflection: A Motorized Sign for the Farm.

Project Examples:

A Very Fast Sign Turner (not geared down—**use as a demo only**)

A Geared Down Sign Turner Using a Worm Gear

Example: Worm Gear Assembly

Parts List:

Name	Picture
Gearbox	
24 tooth spur gear	
Worm Gear	
Axle	
Bushing	

Counting the rotations of a worm gear:

Step 2: Watch this pointer move, stop turning (in step 1) when this pointer returns to the original position.

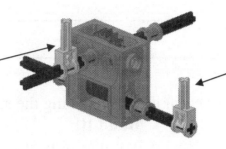

Step 1: Turn this pointer, counting the number of times you turn it one full (360°) turn.

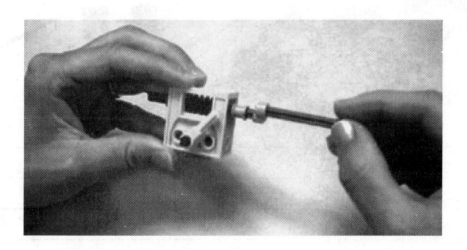

Counting the number of rotations of worm gear
for the spur gear to rotate once

Response Sheet
The Worm Gear

Engineer: _____ Date: _____

Teammate: _____

You can use worm gears to "gear down" reducing the speed of rotation.
Build It!
Build a worm gear using:

Investigate it!
Explore the worm gear & write 3 things you learn about it.

1. _____
   _____
2. _____
   _____
3. _____
   _____

Obtain 2 pointers. Now determine how many times you have to turn the worm gear so that the 24-tooth spur gear turns only **once.**

Write your answer here: _____ times.

For 1 turn of the spur gear

How many times must you turn the worm gear?

Design Sheet
Motorizing the Sign

Engineer: _____ Date: _____

Teammate: _____

1. Prepare a drawing of your design:

```
┌─────────────────────────────────────────┐
│                                           │
│                                           │
│                                           │
│                                           │
│                                           │
│                                           │
│                                           │
│                                           │
│                                           │
│                                           │
│                                           │
│                                           │
│                                           │
│                                           │
│                                           │
│                                           │
│                                           │
└─────────────────────────────────────────┘
```

2. Color the worm gear **yellow**.

3. Write a sentence describing your design.

_____

_____

_____

_____

_____

Response Sheet
Reflection: A Motorized Sign for the Farm

Engineer: _____ Date: _____

Teammate: _____

1. Draw a picture of the gear drive you built for your sign:

```
┌────────────────────────────────────────────────┐
│                                                  │
│                                                  │
│                                                  │
│                                                  │
│                                                  │
│                                                  │
│                                                  │
│                                                  │
│                                                  │
│                                                  │
└────────────────────────────────────────────────┘
```

2. Color the worm gear **yellow**.

3. Study the picture you drew at the beginning of this project. **Reflect on how it differs from what you built. Describe the differences in writing.**

    _____

    _____

    _____

4. Reflect on the gear drive you built. Why did you build it differently from your original design?

    _____

    _____

    _____

Grade Two
Project Six: Motorizing the Tractor

Project Objective: To motorize the tractor using a gear drive connecting the motor to the tractor.

Time: Three to four 45 minute periods

Materials:
- Design Sheet: A Motorized Tractor
- Engineer's Programming Sheet
- Engineer's Two Step Programming Sheet
- LEGO® Mindstorm or Simple Machine kits
- RCX/Battery Pack
- Wire with LEGO® RCX terminals
- Robolab software
- IR Transmitter Tower
- Pre-built tractors from Project Two

Response Sheet:
- Reflection: A Motorized Tractor (Battery Pack)
- Reflection: A Motorized Tractor (RCX)

Vocabulary:
- Motor
- Program
- Robolab
- Icon

Procedure:

The project begins with the teacher asking the students to retrieve their tractors from Project Two and to sit next to their teammate from that building experience. The teacher reviews the design and building processes, asking probing questions about wheels and axles and how they are used to make the tractor move.

The teacher asks the students how they might get the tractor to move using a LEGO® motor with a RCX. Explain that they will be placing a motor and several gears on their tractor drive it. The motor will be connected to the RCX/battery pack for power and control. Using one of the team's pre-built tractors, the teacher models the ideas the students suggest, attaching the motor on the tractor. The teacher models the building process of creating a flat base for the 9-volt motors in order to attach the motor to the tractor securely (Fig. 1)

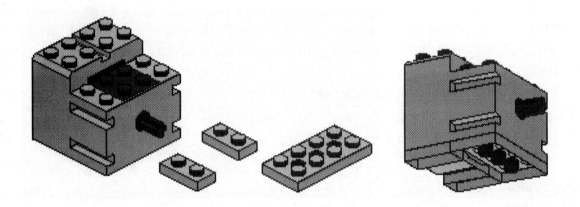

9-volt motor from Mindstorm Kit

9-volt motor from Simple Machine Kit

Fig. 1

He/she also connects the wire with LEGO® RCX terminals from the motor to the RCX/battery pack (Fig. 2). The teacher then runs the motor by pressing run on the RCX/battery pack. The class observes the tractor, noting that it still does not move on its own until the motor is connected to the drive axle.

Battery pack with connecting wire

RCX with connecting wire

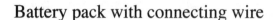

Fig. 2

The teacher then asks the students how they might use their knowledge about gears, and meshing gears, to connect the motor to the axle on their tractor to motorize the tractor. The class discusses how to connect the motor to the driving axle. The teacher then explains that the teams must first prepare a drawing of their design and write a description of their design before they may start building. The teacher gives each student a copy of the Design Sheet: **A Motorized Tractor.**

He/she goes over the sheet with the students and reminds each team that the teacher must approve the design before they begin building it. When the teams have completed their design sheets they should check with the teacher to obtain approval before they are given the LEGO® materials to use.

When the tractors have been motorized, the teams should check again with the teacher and then complete the Response Sheet **Reflection: A Motorized Tractor**.

If you are using a battery pack, the tractors can be displayed for the school community to view.

If you are using an RCX, the teams can begin to program their tractor to start, travel and stop. They will use ROBOLAB software that previously was loaded on a computer to program the RCX. The teacher should give each team a copy of the **Engineer's Programming Sheet** so they can begin programming.

When the teams have completed the Engineer's Programming Sheet with the one step program, they check in with the teacher for instructions on computer use and programming. The teams follow the directions on their programming sheet and test their crane.

The next step in the project is for the teams to create a two step program to move their tractor forward and reverse. The teams should then be given the

Engineer's Two Step Programming Sheet to guide their more advanced programming efforts.

If possible, the motorized tractors should be displayed for the school community to view. They can then be disassembled at a convenient time. Students will be instructed on the care of LEGO® materials and to sort and store these materials.

Extensions:

- Add a touch sensor to the tractor. Program (in Pilot 3) the tractor to wait for the touch sensor to be activated (switch button pushed in) before it runs.

Assessment:

- Completion of the Design Sheet: **A Motorized Tracto**r.
- Completion of the Response Sheet: **Reflection: A Motorized Tractor.**
- Completion of the challenges with teacher interviews and observations.
- Completion of the Response Sheet: **Engineer's Programming Sheet.**
- Completion of the Response Sheet: **Engineer's Two Step Programming Sheet.**
- Successful programming of the tractor to move forward and backward.

Teacher's Programming Guide:

The students will program their tractors to move forward for a specified amount of time by using Pilot One of the ROBOLAB software. Students should first plan their program using the **Engineering Programming Sheet** and the **Programmer's Icon Sheet**.

After planning their program on paper, the students should:

- Click on the "Programmer" icon after opening up the software (Fig. 3).

Fig. 3

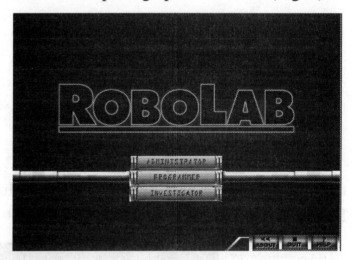

- Then double click on "Pilot One" (Fig. 4).

Fig. 4

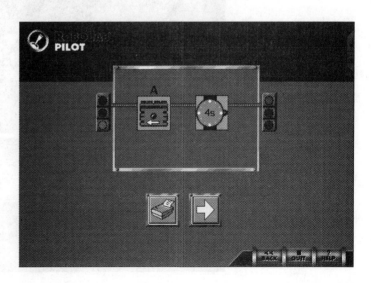

- By holding down an icon with the mouse button, the students can change the selection on the screen. They can choose different amounts of time such as 1, 2, 4, 6, 8 or ? seconds

- When they have finished selecting the program, the students can click on the white arrow (Fig. 5) under the icons to download their program on the RCX. The RCX should be placed next to the IR Tower. The RCX should be turned on before downloading.

Fig. 5

- They should then run their program to see if it downloads correctly.

- The students should repeat these steps another time, changing the amount of time the tractor moves.

After successful completion of Pilot One programming, the students should then use the Pilot Three program (Fig. 6). In Pilot Three, the students should program their tractor to move forward and back for a specific amount of time.

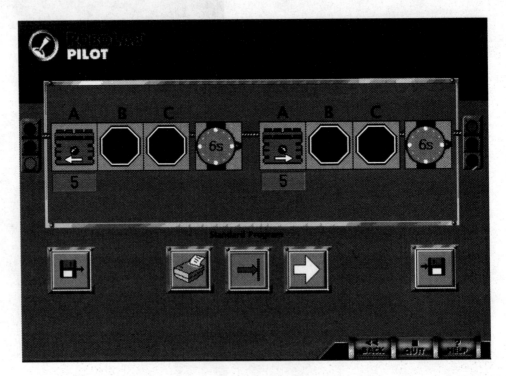

Fig. 6

Sample Building Projects

Motorized Tractor

Internals views of motor and pulley systems

Meshed gears connecting the motor to the drive axle

LEGO® plates are used under the motor to get a perfect mesh of the gears from the motor to the drive axle.

Design Sheet
A Motorized Tractor

Engineer: _____ Date: _____

Teammate: _____

Challenge: Using a LEGO® motor and meshed gears motorize the tractor from Wilbur's barn.

1. Prepare a drawing of your design.

2. Color the gears **red** in your drawing.

3. Color the motor **blue** in your drawing.

4. Describe your design in writing:

_____

_____

_____

5. Now share your plans with your teammate. Combine ideas and concepts from both team members into your tractor design.

6. Check in with your teacher and obtain her approval of your design before you begin building.

Response Sheet
Reflection: A Motorized Tractor (Battery Pack)

Engineer: _____ Date: _____

Teammate: _____

1. Prepare a drawing of the tractor you built:

[blank box]

2. Color the gears **red**.

3. Color the motor **blue**.

4. Reflect on your building. Examine the picture you drew at the beginning of this project. Why did you build your motorized tractor differently from what you originally designed?

_____

_____

_____

_____

Response Sheet
Reflection: A Motorized Tractor (RCX)

Engineer: _____ Date: _____

Teammate: _____

    1. Prepare a drawing of the tractor you built:

    2. Color the gears **red**.

    3. Color the motor **blue**.

    4. Reflect on your building. Examine the picture you drew at the beginning of this project. Why did you build your motorized tractor differently from what you originally designed?

    _____

    _____

    _____

    _____

    5. Now check with your teacher for programming instructions.

Engineer's Programming Sheet

Engineer: _____ Date: _____
Teammate: _____

Your programming challenge is to move your tractor forward for 1, 2, 4, 6, 8, or ? seconds.

1. Discuss the time with your teammate and decide on the time.

2. Complete this sentence by recording your decision.
   Our tractor will move forward for _____ seconds.

3. Using the icons on the **Programmer's Icon Sheet** cut and paste the icons you plan to use in your program.

Program 1: Our tractor will go forward for _____ seconds.

4. Now check with your teacher to receive his/her instructions on how to program. You will be assigned a computer to use.

- Select "Programmer" when ROBOLAB opens.
- Double click on "Pilot One" to program.
- When finished put your RCX next to the IR Tower.
- Turn on your RCX.
- Click the big white arrow on Pilot One screen.

5. When you are successful with programming your time of motion, write a different program with a different time. Complete the sentence:

　　　　Now our tractor will now move forward _____ seconds

6. Cut and paste the icons for this new program.

Program 2: Our tractor will go forward for _____ seconds.

7. Now use the computer to program your tractor for this new time.

- Hold down the icon for time
- Select a different time

8. Reflect on your programming. Write **one programming tip** that other students might find helpful when they are programming.

_____

_____

_____

_____

_____

_____

Engineer's Two Step Programming Sheet

Engineer: _____ Date: _____

Teammate: _____

Your new programming challenge is: To move your tractor forward for 1, 2, 4, 6, or 8 seconds and then move it in reverse for a different number of seconds. This forward and reverse motion requires a two step program.

1. Discuss the time with your teammate and decide on it.
2. Complete this sentence.

Our tractor will move forward _____ seconds and then move in reverse _____ seconds.

3. Using the icons on the **Programmer's Icon Sheet** cut and paste the icons to plan out your program.

Program 1: Our tractor will go forward for _____ seconds and in reverse for _____ seconds. .

4. Now check in with your teacher for instructions on how select this program on the computer. You will be assigned a computer to use.

   - Select "Programmer" when ROBOLAB opens
   - Double click on "Pilot Three" to open the program.
   - Create the program on the screen by selecting the icons that match the icons on paper program you created.
   - When finished put your RCX next to the IR Tower.
   - Turn your RCX on.
   - Click the big white arrow on Pilot Three screen.
   - Wait while the program loads on to your RCX.
   - Run your RCX.

5. When you are successful with your time, try a different program with different times.

6. Reflect on your programming in Pilot Three. How was Pilot Three different from Pilot One?

   _____

   _____

   _____

   _____

   _____

7. Write **one programming tip** that other students might find helpful when they are programming in Pilot 3.

   _____

   _____

   _____

   _____

   _____

Programmer's Icon Sheet

Cut and paste the icon desired on your Engineering Programming Sheet

Motors:

Forward

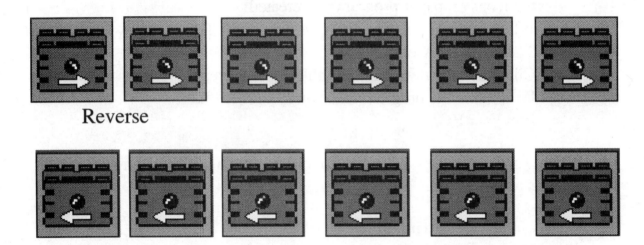

Reverse

Time:

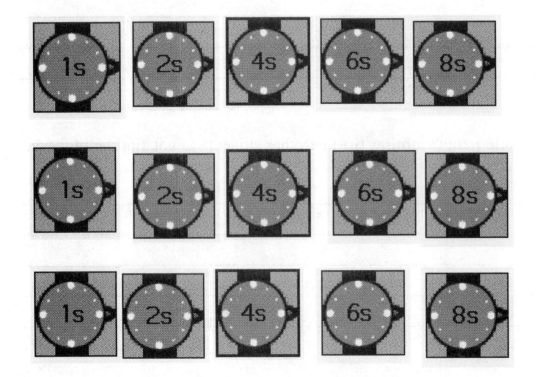

Grade Two
Project Seven: A Snail Robot

Project Objective: To design, build, test, redesign and retest a snail robot that demonstrates double gear drive to reduce the robot's speed.

Time: Three to four 45 minute periods

Materials:
- LEGO® Mindstorm or Simple Machine kits
- Worm gear in gear box
- RCX
- Wire with LEGO® RCX terminals
- Art supplies to embellish snails
- Interactive whiteboard or chart paper mounted on an easel
- Class Data Table displayed on an interactive whiteboard or on chart paper mounted on an easel for students to fill in (for reflection)

Response sheets:
- Exploring Gears
- Designing a Snail Robot
- Snail Robots: How fast do they go?
- Reflection: Snail Robots
- Extension: Estimating with Snail Robots

Vocabulary:
- Geared down
- Gear drive
- Average

Procedure:

The project begins with students reviewing what it means to gear down a gear train, a concept explored in Project Three in the Grade Two Projects. The teacher leads a discussion reviewing gears, the vocabulary associated with gears and what it means to gear down a gear train. The students then review the concepts by completing the Response Sheet: **Exploring Gears**. The teacher assembles the class to share their learning experiences. He/she directs the discussion on what it might mean to gear down a robot.

The teacher introduces the challenge: to build a snail robot from LEGO® components that moves very slowly. The snail robots must include a motor, gears and a space for the RCX. The robots must move as slowly as possible, trying to gear it down enough to travel a twelve inch space in more than a minute.

The students are divided into teams of two and given the Response Sheet: **Snail Robots: Designing a Snail Robot** to complete before they begin building. The class goes over the sheet.

The teacher asks the class to think about how they might test their robots to see how slowly they actually move. The class discusses how they will measure the distance the robot travels and how they will measure the time it takes for the robot to travel that distance. The teacher displays the response sheet: **Snail Robots: How fast do they go?** The class goes over the response sheet, discussing how to measure the distance and the speed of their trials. The teacher instructs the class on how to record the data in the table. The teacher then asks if anyone knows what an average is. He/she discusses what this means, recording a class definition on the interactive whiteboard or on the chart paper. The teacher then explains how the team will find the average for their three trails. When they are finished they will record their average on the Class data table on the easel (Fig. 1)

Name of Snail Robot	Average Speed from Test 1(seconds)

Fig. 1 Class Data Table

The teams are instructed to check in with the teacher when their design sheets are completed. When the teams complete this Response Sheet, they are given LEGO® building materials to begin their project and build a robotic snail.

When teams are finished building and ready to test their robot, and measure its speed, the teacher gives them a copy of the Response Sheet: **Snail Robots: How fast do they go?** to complete. The team begins by naming their robot. They then test the speed of the robot by timing how long it takes the robot to travel a twelve inch distance. They record their findings on the data table on the response sheet. They repeat the test two more times, recording their time of their trials on their data table. The team then computes the average speed for their three trials.

Set up a class data table on the interactive whiteboard or on the chart paper mounted on an easel. As teams finish testing their snail robots, they should record their data on to the class data table. When all of the entries have been made on the Table, calculate the snail robot's average speed and share it with the class.

When most teams have nearly finished building, give the class a time deadline for completion of the testing of their snail robot. At the designated time, bring the class together for sharing of their work. Ask each team to introduce the design feature used to build their robot snail, report on its speed and demonstrate how it moves. Ask teams to discuss a problem they encountered when building the snail robot and what they did to solve it. At the end of the class discussion, give the students the Response Sheet: **Reflection: Snail Robots** and **Self Evaluation** to complete as a final evaluation.

If possible, the snail robots should be displayed for the school community to view. The robots can then be disassembled at a convenient time. Students will be instructed on the care of LEGO® materials and to sort and store these materials.

Extensions:

- Completion of the Response Sheet: Extension: Estimating with Snail Robots.

Assessment:

- Successful completion of the Response Sheet: Exploring Gears
- Successful completion of the Response Sheet: Designing a Snail Robot
- Successful design and building of a snail robot that demonstrates a double gear drive to reduce speed
- Self Evaluation: Simple Machines: Gears

Example of a Gearing Down Assembly for robot:

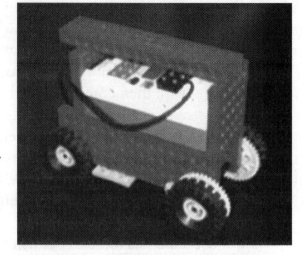

The RCX can slide in and out of this car in the space provided by its rectangular frame.

Examine the geared down spur gears. The small gear is a pinion and the large one is sometimes called a bull gear.

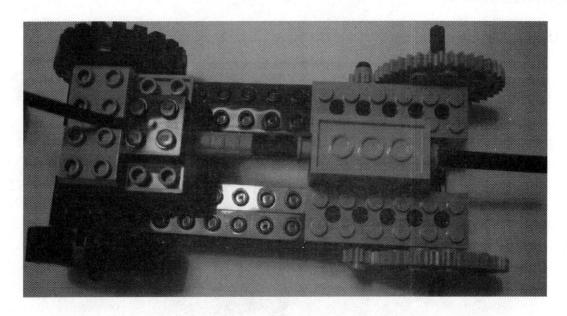

An inside view of a drive with a worm gear

Other examples for your consideration in designing your gear drives:

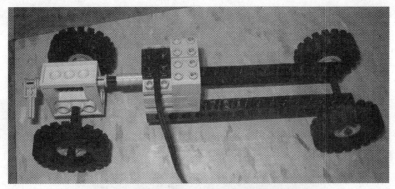

Project Examples:

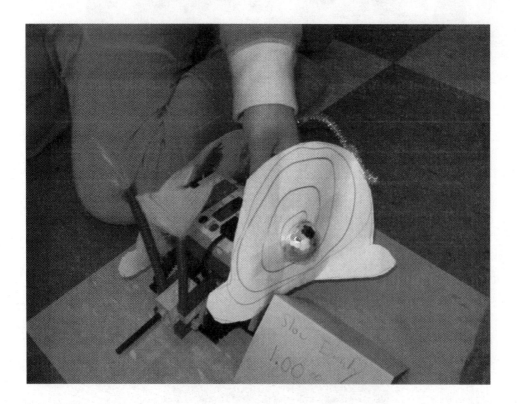

Response Sheet
Exploring Gears

Engineer: _____Date: _____

Teammate: _____

Explore the gears on the tray.

1. Draw two gears in mesh that show the **follower geared down.**

How many times slower is the follower than the driver? _____

2. Can you find other examples of gears in mesh that are **geared down**? Prepare a drawing of them:

Response Sheet
Designing a Snail Robot

Engineer: _____ Date: _____

Teammate: _____

We will be building **snail like robots**. We will use what we have learned about gears to "gear down" a robot to make it go as slowly as possible—at a snail's pace. Your snail robot must:

- Be able to travel 1 foot (1 floor tile) in more than 60 seconds
- Be geared down
- Use one motor
- Use a worm gear
- Have a space in which to slide and hold the RCX

With your partner, discuss some ideas you have about designing and building your robot.

- Use ideas from both teammates.
- Prepare a drawing of your design that you plan to build.

What will you add to make your robot look like a snail?

_____

_____

Response Sheet
Snail Robots: How fast do they go?

Engineer: _____Date: _____

Teammate: _____

1. Test your snail robot to measure its speed. Measure how many seconds it takes your snail robot to travel 1 floor tile, or 1 foot. Record the time on the data table.

Snail's name: _____

First test	Time (sec)
#1	
#2	
#3	
Average	

2. What could you change on your robot's design to make it go even slower?

_____

_____

3. Try your new design (idea) and then retest your robot. Complete the table below with your new data.

Second test	Time (sec)
#1	
#2	
#3	
Average	

Response Sheet
Extension: Estimating with Snail Robots

Engineer: _____Date: _____

Teammate: _____

1. Measure your robot's speed. Complete the data table.

Distance traveled	Time (in seconds)
1 foot	
2 feet	
3 feet	

2. Estimate how much time it would take your snail to go 10 feet. _____.

3. Test it: how much time did it take? _____ **Add** the data to your table.

4. Create a point-line graph of your robot's speed. Prepare a graph showing the time for the robot to move 1, 2, 3 and 10 feet.

5. Using your graph, answer the following questions.

   a. Describe the shape of your graph.

   _____

   _____

   b. What is the average speed of your robot snail over a distance of 5 feet? _____ Describe how you determined this number from the graph.

   _____

   _____

   c. Now test your robot by running it a distance of 5 feet. What time did you measure? _____ Was it the same or different from your answer to question b? _____ Why do you think the difference occurred?

   _____

Response Sheet
Reflection: Snail Robots

Engineer: _____ Date: _____

Teammate: _____

Data Table of Snail Robots average speed:
- Copy the data from the easel onto this data table.

Name of Snail Robot	Average Speed from Test 1(seconds)

Reflect on the experience of building of your snail robot.

1. What was one **problem** you encountered when building your snail?

_____

_____

2. How did you **solve** this problem?

_____

_____

_____

3. Examine the data table. Write one fact comparing the data from two teams.

_____

_____

Response Sheet
Self Evaluation: Simple Machines: Gears

Engineer: _____ Date: _____

Take a few minutes and consider the experiences that helped you learn about gears and gear drives. Check the learning grid on your opinion.

My Learning behavior	Always	Sometimes	Hardly ever
I listened carefully.			
I worked carefully.			
I wrote down my ideas.			
I listened to others.			
I shared materials.			
I cleaned up.			

Write one thing you are proud of in this project:

_____

_____

Write two facts you learned about gears:

_____

_____

_____

Write three words that describe gears:

_____

_____

_____

Grade Two
Project Eight: Pulley Power

Project Objective: To familiarized the students with pulleys and to design and build a simple pulley system

Time: Three to four 45 minute periods

Materials:
- LEGO® Mindstorm or Simple Machine kits
- Light object for lifting
- Pulley Assessment Sheet
- Pictures of pulleys from other sources

Response Sheet:
- Exploring Pulleys
- Exploring More Pulleys
- Pulleys That Move Things

Vocabulary:
- Pulley wheel- special wheel with a grooved rim that holds a belt or rope
- Belt
- Driver—pulley wheel starting the motion
- Follower—pulley wheel following the driver

Procedure:

Prior to beginning the project, the teachers should find pictures of pulleys and bring them class. The project begins with the teacher leading a discussion about pulleys. The teacher should display different pictures of pulleys in action. The teacher may ask questions such as:

- Why do people use pulleys?
- How do pulleys work?
- How do you think you would build a pulley?

Next, the teacher shows the students a diagram of a pulley (Fig. 1 & 2) with the new vocabulary building words: pulley wheel; driver; follower; and pulley belt.

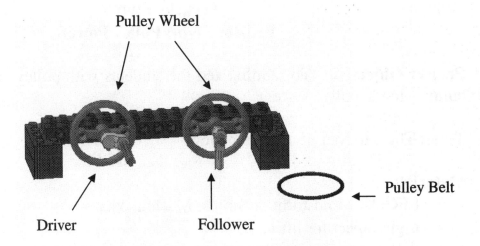

Pulley Wheel

Pulley Belt

Driver   Follower

Fig. 1

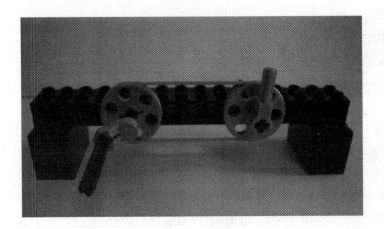

Fig. 2

The teacher demonstrates how to attach the pulley belt to the pulley wheels and turns the driver pulley for the class to observe the effect.

The teacher introduces the project. He/she explains that they will be working as a team. They will be building and exploring the pulleys together, completing the Response Sheet: **Exploring Pulleys** as they work. Give each student a Response Sheet: **Exploring Pulleys**. Review the Response Sheet, answering any questions that the students might have.

Students then begin the project. When the student teams finish **Exploring Pulleys**, the teacher checks their Response Sheets for accuracy and completeness. He/she then gives them the next Response Sheet: **Exploring More Pulleys** to complete. After completing both Response Sheets, the teacher leads a class discussion about the project with questions such as:

- What is something new that you learned about pulleys?
- Have you seen any pulleys similar to the models you designed and built?
- What was your power source for turning the pulleys?
- How did you make the follower move in the same direction as the driver? Move it in the opposite directions than the driver?
- What did you do to make the follower move faster than the driver? Move it slower than the driver?

Next the teacher introduces the final part of the project, pulleys that use ropes instead of belts. He/she explains that they will be working with the same teammate as in the last two activities. They will be designing, building and exploring the pulleys together, completing the Response Sheet while they work. Give each student a Response Sheet: **Pulleys That Move Things**. After the teacher reviews the Response Sheet for the class, the students work as teams to complete the activity. When all the students have completed the Response Sheet, the teacher leads a concluding discussion summarizing the facts learned during this project.

The pulley models will be dissembled at the conclusion of the project. Students will be instructed on the care of LEGO® materials and to sort and store the pieces. The **Pulley Assessment** sheet should be distributed at the end of the project.

Extensions:

- Students can motorize the pulley

Assessment:

- Completion of the Response Sheet: **Exploring Pulleys**.
- Completion of the Response Sheet: **Exploring More Pulleys**.
- Completion of the Response Sheet: **Pulleys That Move Things.**
- Completion of the **Pulley Assessment Sheet**
- Teacher observations and interviews

Teacher's Notes:

Answer key to Exploring Pulleys

1. Build a pulley model that looks like this. Add a belt to connect both pulleys.

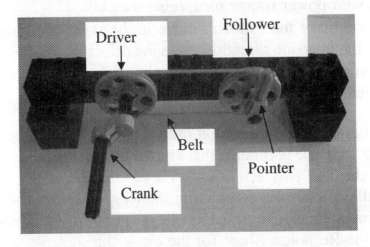

2. On the picture above, label the following parts:

   Driver; Follower; Belt; Crank; Pointer

3. Predict what will happen when you rotate the driver clockwise.

4. Rotate the driver clockwise. Describe in writing what you observed.

   Answer: The follower rotates clockwise.

5. Try rotating either the driver or the follower clockwise and note that both pulleys rotate in the clockwise direction.

6. What can you do to the model to make the pulleys to rotate in different directions?

   Answer: Cross the pulley belt

7. Try crossing the belt as shown on the figure below. Draw the change you made to the belt that made the pulleys rotate in different directions.

On your drawing label the following parts:

- Driver
- Follower
- Belt
- Crank
- Pointer

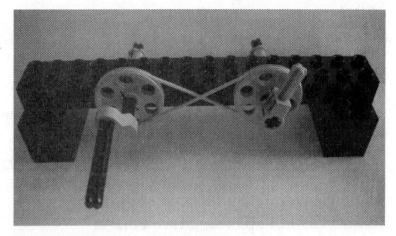

8. Replace the driver with a bushing pulley so your model looks like the one shown below:

9. Which pulley rotates faster?

   Answer: Driver

10. Why do you think this pulley rotates faster?

   Answer: It is smaller.

11. What could you do to the model to get the follower to rotate faster?

   Answer: Reverse it. Use the small pulley as the follower.

12. Try this arrangement. Prepare a drawing showing what you did to make the follower move faster.

13. Describe in writing some fact that you learned about pulleys.

Answer: Some second grade thoughts about pulleys:

- Pulleys rotate things.
- Pulleys connect each other by a pulley belt.
- The driver pulley turns the same direction as the follower pulley.
- When you cross the pulley belt, the pulleys move in opposite directions.
- You can speed up or slow down a pulley by using a smaller one than its mate.

Answer key to Exploring More Pulleys

1. Build a pulley model with two belts that looks like the one shown below:

2. How is this model different from the ones you built before?

Answer: The model has two sets of pulleys

3. Rotate the driver. Describe what happens to the other pulleys in this model?
Answer: The other pulleys turn in the same direction as the driver. The larger pulley turns slower than the smaller pulleys.

4. What use would you make of a pulley system?

5. Now build the model shown to the below.

 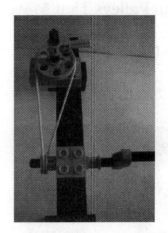

Side view   Top view

6. How is this pulley different from the ones you built before?

   Answer: The follower pulley is set 90° from the driver pulley. Its orientation has changed from horizontal to vertical. The pulley band twists.

7. Rotate the driver. Describe what happens to the other pulley in this model?

Answer: The follower pulley turns in the same direction as the driver but 90° (or vertical) from the (horizontal) driver pulley, with motion similar to what we did with the crown gear in lesson four.

8. What might be a good use for this type of pulley system?

Answer: a chair lift at a ski slope

9. Describe in writing some fact that you learned about pulleys.

   Answers:

   • Driver pulleys can be connected together with pulley bands to turn more than one follower pulley.
   • Pulleys can be built in line with each other or at other orientations to each other.
   • The orientation of the follower pulley can be changed from horizontal to vertical or east to west.

Answer key to Pulleys That Move Things

1. Build a pulley model that looks like the one shown below:

2. Using other LEGO® pieces, create a hook at the end of the string so that you can attach something to the string to lift it. Here is an example. Can you think of other ways for lifting?

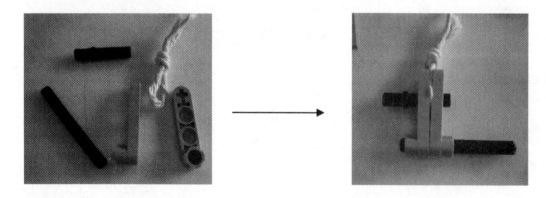

3. Predict what will happen if you turn the crank and pull the string.

   Answer: The pulley belt is a pulley rope.

4. Try it! Hold your pulley in your hand and use it to lift something light in your classroom. Describe how your pulley worked.

5. How is this pulley system different from the other ones you built?

Answer: This model uses a pulley to lift things.

6. What use could be made of this pulley system?

Answer: This model could lift things.

7. Describe how this pulley could be changed to make it more useful in lifting things.

Answer: This model could be attached to other beams and placed on a table top for easier lifting.

Response Sheet
Exploring Pulleys

Engineer: _____ Date: _____

Teammate: _____

1. Build a pulley model that looks like the one shown below. Add the pulley belt to connect both pulleys.

2. On the photograph above, label the following parts:

   Driver; Follower; Belt; Crank; Pointer

3. Predict what happens when you rotate the driver clockwise:

   _____

   _____

4. Rotate the driver clockwise. Describe in writing what you observed.

   _____

   _____

5. Do the two pulleys rotate in the same direction or different directions?

   ☐   Same direction   ☐   Different direction

6. What changes could you make to the model for the pulleys to rotate in different directions?

_____

_____

7. Try your change. Prepare a drawing showing the change you made so the pulleys rotated in different directions. In your drawing label the driver, follower and belt.

8. Replace the driver with a bushing pulley so your model looks like the one shown to the right. Add a belt to connect the bushing pulley to the pulley.

9. Which pulley moves faster?

☐ Driver ☐ Follower

10. Why do you think the small pulley moves faster?

_____

_____

_____

_____

11. What changes could you make for the follower to rotate faster?

_____

_____

_____

_____

12. Try your changes. Prepare a drawing showing the changes you made that caused the follower to rotate faster. In your drawing label the driver, follower and belt.

13. Describe in writing some fact or facts that you learned about pulleys.

_____

_____

_____

_____

_____

Response Sheet
Exploring More Pulleys

Engineer: _____ Date: _____

Teammate: _____

1. Build a pulley model with two belts that looks like the one shown below:

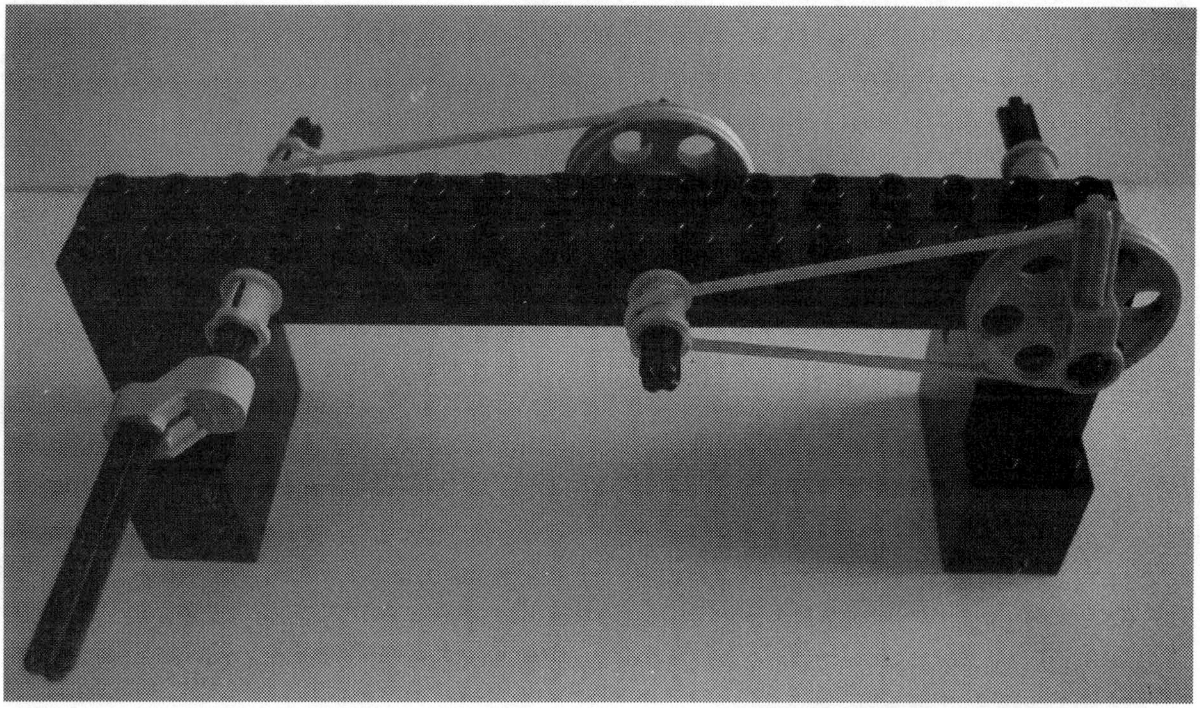

2. How is this model different from the ones you built before?

_____

_____

_____

3. Rotate the driver. Describe what happens to the other pulleys in this model?

_____

_____

_____

_____

4. What use would you make of a pulley system?

_____

_____

_____

_____

5. Now build the model shown to the below.

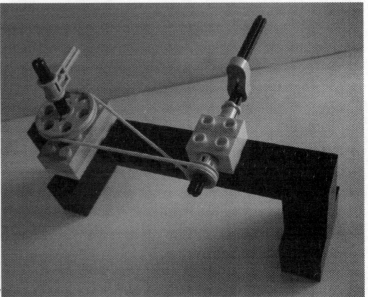

Oblique View

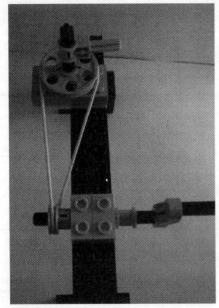

Top view

6. How does this pulley different from the ones you built before?

_____

_____

_____

7. Rotate the driver. Describe what happens to the other pulley in this model?

_____

_____

_____

_____

8. What might be a good use for this type of pulley system?

_____

_____

_____

9. Describe in writing some fact that you learned about pulleys.

_____

_____

_____

Response Sheet
Pulleys That Move Things

Engineer: _____ Date: _____

Teammate: _____

1. Build a pulley model that looks like the one shown below: This is a hand held model. You will need:

LEGO® piece	Number needed
1x 16 beam	2
1x 6 beam	1
2 x 6 plate	1
Hubs	3
12 stud axle	1
10 stud axle	1
4 stud axle	1
Crank	1
Bushing	5
String	About 12 inches

Side view

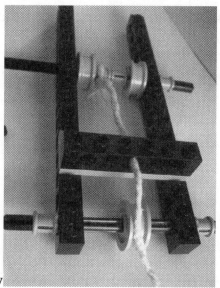

Front View

2. Using other LEGO® pieces, create a hook at the end of the string so that you can attach something to the string to lift it. Here is an example. Can you think of other ways of doing this task?

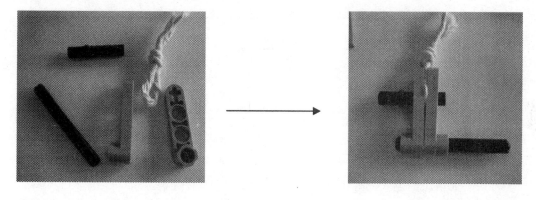

3. Predict what will happen if you turn the crank and pull the string.

_____

_____

4. Try it! Hold your pulley in your hand and use it to lift something light in your classroom. Describe how your pulley worked.

_____

_____

_____

_____

5. How is this pulley system different from the other ones you built?

_____

_____

_____

_____

6. What use could be made of this pulley system?

_____

_____

_____

7. Describe how this pulley could be changed to make it more useful in lifting things.

_____

_____

_____

Examples of cranes using pulley systems for lifting heavy objects.

Pulley Assessment

Engineer: _____ Date: _____

Consider what you learned during the pulley project. Check the learning grid to show your learning behavior.

My Learning behavior.....	Always	Sometimes	Never
I listened carefully.			
I wrote down my ideas.			
I listened to others.			
I shared materials.			
I cleaned up.			

One thing I would use a pulley for:

_____

_____

Two things I learned about pulleys:

_____

_____

Imagine you are on this sailboat. On the back side of this paper, draw a pulley system that helps you raise and lower the sail.

Grade Two
Project Nine: Building a Crane

Project Objective: To design and build a crane equipped with a pulley system capable of lifting a large load.

Time: Three to four 45 minute periods

Materials:
- Pictures of cranes lifting different kind of loads
- LEGO® Mindstorm or Simple Machine kits
- Building Design Sheet: **Designing a Crane**
- Book—Charlotte's Web by E. B. White
- A stuffy or a similar item to lift

Response Sheet:
- Reflection: Building a Crane

Vocabulary:
- Pulley wheel
- Pulley rope or belt
- Load
- Driver
- Follower

Procedure:

The teacher begins the project by leading a discussion about pulleys. He/she reviews the names and parts of a pulley system. The teacher may ask questions such as:

- Has anyone used a pulley at home?
- What jobs are easier because of pulleys?
- Where have you seen pulleys used in your community?
- What structures have pulleys in them?

The class then reviews the crane models the children built from the Project 8: **Pulley Power**. The teacher asks the students what we lifted in that model.

He/she then introduces the word **load** and asks the students to consider other types of loads that cranes might lift. The teacher shares pictures of cranes, asking questions about each one to help the students visualize what they will design, draw and build.

The students are presented with the building project which is to build a crane that can lift a large load. The teacher asks the students what types of loads they might want to lift. He/she should direct their thoughts to the book **Charlotte's Web** and the items they might want to lift on a farm or at a fair. The students are divided into teams of two and given the Response Sheet: **Designing a Crane.** He/she goes over the sheet with the students and reminds each team that the teacher must approve the design before they begin building it. The teams are instructed to draw a crane that they might build using LEGO® building pieces. The teams should check with the teacher to obtain his/her approval before they begin to build their crane.

The teams work at their own pace, when building the crane. When completed, the teams should use their crane to lift a load (such as Wilber the beanie baby, LEGO® people, blocks, etc).

When the teams have completed building their crane, they should present their crane to the class, sharing their successes and challenges. Encourage the students to share how they solved their problems.

If possible, the cranes should be displayed for the school community to view until they are needed for Project Ten.

The response sheet **Reflection: Building a Crane** should be distributed at the end of the project.

Extensions:
- Students add a cab to the crane to shelter a worker
- Students build a container to hold a load of pennies

Assessment:
- Building a working model of a crane using a pulley system
- Completion of the Building Design Sheet: **Designing a Crane**
- Completion of the Response Sheet: **Reflection: Building a Crane."**
- Teacher observations and interviews

Sample Building Projects

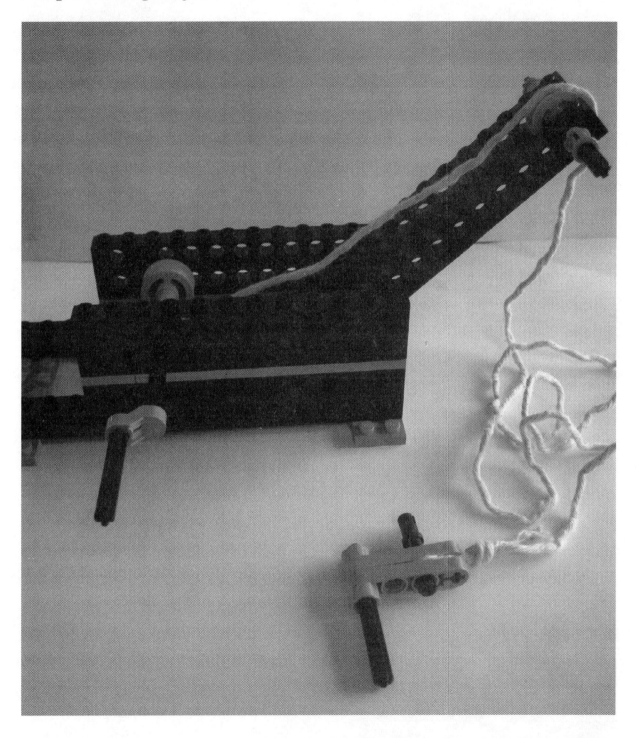

Crane with hook

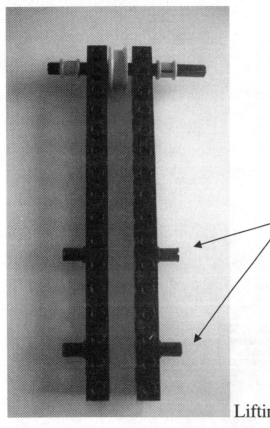

Friction pegs are used to securely attach lifting arm to support structure.

Lifting arm of the crane

Friction pegs attach arm to support structure.

Pulley rope is tied to the axle that turns.

Building Design Sheet
Designing a Crane

Engineer: _____ Date: _____

Teammate: _____

With your partner, discuss some ideas you have about designing and building a crane.

- Use ideas from both teammates.
- Prepare a drawing of your design that you plan to build.

1. Prepare a drawing of your design (idea):

2. Color the pulley red.

3. Write the word load next to the object your crane will be lifting.

4. Describe your design in writing:

_____

_____

_____

Response Sheet
Reflection: Building a Crane

Engineer: _____ Date: _____

Teammate: _____

1.   Prepare a drawing of the crane you built:

2. Color the pulley **red.**

3. Examine the picture you drew at the beginning of this project. Reflect on how it is different from what you built. Discuss in writing some of your thoughts.

    _____

    _____

    _____

4. Reflect on your building. Why did you build your crane differently from what you originally thought you would build?

    _____

    _____

Grade Two
Project Ten: Motorize a Crane

Project Objective: To motorize the crane (from Project Nine) using a geared system that has been geared down.

Time: Two to three 45 minute periods

Materials:
- LEGO® Mindstorm or Simple Machine kits
- Worm gear in a gear box
- RCX
- Wire with LEGO® RCX terminals
- Building Design Sheet: Motorizing a Crane
- Engineer's Programming Sheet
- Book—Charlotte's Web by E. B. White
- A stuffy or a similar item to lift

Response Sheet:
- Reflection: A Motorized Crane

Vocabulary:
- worm gear
- gear down
- pulley wheel
- pulley rope or belt
- axle extender

Procedure:

The project begins with the teacher asking the students to retrieve their cranes from Project Nine and to sit next to their teammate from that building experience. The teacher begins the class with a review of the vocabulary from that building project, which includes: pulley; pulley rope; load; driver and follower.

The teacher holds up a worm gear in the gear box and reviews the worm gear (see Project Five), asking the students to share some of the things they remember about the worm gear. He/she reviews how to assemble the worm gear in the gear box and how to attach the gear box to a motor. The teacher also reviews what it means to gear down an object, reminding the students of the rotating signs from Project Five.

The teacher asks the students to think about how they might motorize the cranes they built in the last project using a motor and the worm gear in the gear box. The cranes will need to be geared down to slow them down. The motorized crane will be powered by the RCX. The class shares ideas.

Each student is given the **Response Sheet: Motorizing a Crane.** The teacher goes over the sheet with the students and reminds each team that the teacher must approve the design before they begin building it. The teams are instructed to draw a motorized crane that they might build using worm gears; motors and LEGO® building pieces. The teams should check with the teacher to obtain his/her approval before they begin to build.

When the cranes have been motorized, the teams should check in again with the teacher and complete the response sheet **Reflection Sheet: A Motorized Crane**.

If you are using an RCX, the teams can begin to program their cranes to lift a load. They will use ROBOLAB software that previously was loaded on a computer to program the RCX. The teacher should give each team a copy of the **Engineer's Programming Sheet** and the **Programmer's Icon Sheet** so they can begin programming.

When the teams have completed the **Engineer's Programming Sheet** with the one step program, they check in with the teacher for instructions on computer use and programming. The teams follow the directions on their programming sheet and test their crane.

The next step in the project is for the teams to create a two step program to move their crane up and down. The teams should then be given the **Engineer's Two Step Programming Sheet** to guide their more advanced programming efforts. They will also use the **Programmer's Icon Sheet** previously given to them.

After the students have finished building and programming their crane, the teams should share their crane model, sharing some of the successes and some of the problems they had in their building and programming. Teams are encouraged to share some of their problem solving techniques.

If possible, the motorized cranes should be displayed for the school community to view. They can then be disassembled at a convenient time. Students will be instructed on the care of LEGO® materials and to sort and store these materials.

Extensions:

- Students slow the motor down even more using different size pulleys.
- Students add & program a touch sensor to start the movement of the crane.

Assessment:

- Building a working model of a motorized crane
- Successful programming of the crane with specifics movements
- Completion of the Building Design Sheet: Designing a Motorized Crane
- Completion of the Response Sheet: Reflection: A Motorized Crane
- Teacher observations and interviews

Teacher's Programming Guide:

The students will program their cranes to move for a specified amount of time by using Pilot One of the ROBOLAB software. Students should first plan their program using the **Engineering Programming Sheet** and the **Programmer's Icon Sheet**.

After planning their program on paper, the students should:

- Click on the "Programmer" icon after opening up the software (Fig. 1).

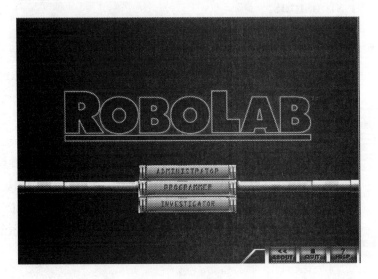

Fig. 1

- Then double click on "Pilot One" (Fig. 2). In this program motor A runs for 4 seconds and stops.

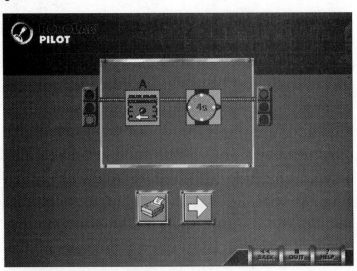

Fig. 2

- By holding down an icon with the mouse button, the students can change the selection on the screen. They can choose different amounts of time such as 1, 2, 4, 6, 8 or ? seconds.

- When they have finished selecting the program, the students can click on the white arrow (Fig. 3) under the icons to download their program on the RCX. The RCX should be placed next to the IR Tower. The RCX should be turned on before pressing the arrow for downloading the program.

Fig. 3

- The students should then run their program to see if it downloads correctly.

- The students should repeat these steps another time, changing the amount of time the tractor moves.

After successful completion of Pilot One programming, the students should then use the Pilot Three program (Fig. 4). In Pilot Three, the students should program their crane to move forward and back for a specific amount of time. In this program, motor A runs in one direction for 6 seconds and then in reverse for 6 seconds. The motors are powered with a setting of 5.

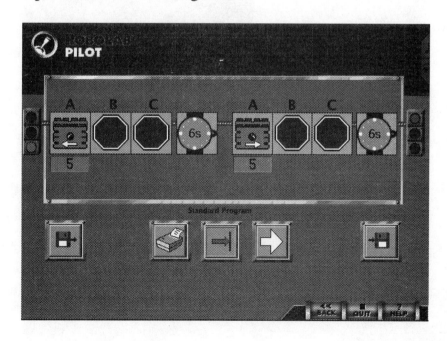

Fig. 4

Project Examples:

Crane is motorized and geared down by using a worm gear

Close up view of motor and worm gear

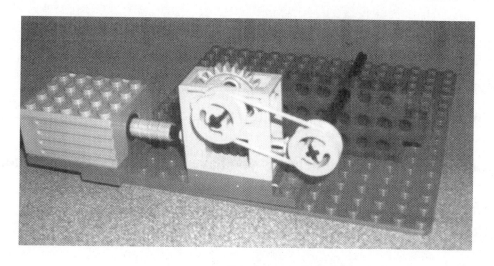

Worm gear connected with a pulley

Worm gear geared down

Building Design Sheet: A Motorized Crane

Engineer: _____ Date: _____

Teammate: _____

With your partner, discuss some ideas you have about motorizing a crane.

- Use ideas from both teammates.
- Prepare a drawing of your design that you plan to build.

1. Prepare a drawing of your design (idea):

2. Color the pulleys **red** in your drawing.

3. Color the motor **blue** in your drawing.

4. Color the worm gear **yellow** in your drawing.

5. Describe your design in writing:

_____

_____

_____

_____

Reflection: A Motorized Crane

Engineer: _____ Date: _____

Teammate: _____

1. Prepare a drawing of the crane you built:

2. Color the pulley **red,** the motor **blue** and the worm gear **yellow** in your drawing.

3. Examine the picture you drew at the beginning of this project. Reflect on how it is different from what you built. Discuss in writing some of your thoughts.

   _____

   _____

   _____

4. Reflect on your building. Why did you motorize your crane differently from what you originally thought you would do?

   _____

   _____

   _____

Engineer's Programming Sheet

Engineer: _____ Date: _____

Teammate: _____

Your programming challenge is to lift the load on your crane for **4 seconds**.

1. Using the icons on the **Programmer's Icon Sheet** cut and paste the icons to plan out your program. The first program is to have our crane's motor lifting for 4 seconds.

2. Now check in with your teacher for instructions on how to program. You will be assigned a computer to use. To program in Robolab:

   - Select "Programmer" when ROBOLAB opens
   - Double click on "Pilot One" to program.
   - Create a program on the screen by selecting the icon that matches the icon on your paper program.
   - When finished creating the electronic program, place your RCX next to the IR Tower.
   - Turn your RCX on by pressing the red on/off button.
   - Click the big white arrow on Pilot One screen.
   - Wait while the program loads on to your RCX.
   - Run your RCX.

When you are successful with programming your time of motion, write a second program with a different lifting time. Complete the sentence:

The load on our crane will be lifted for _____ seconds.

3. Cut and paste the icons for this new program.

The new program: Our crane's motor will lift for _____ seconds.

4. Now use the computer to program your tractor for this new time.

- Hold down the icon for time
- Select a different time
- Download the new program on to your RCX
- Run the program

5 Reflect on your programming. Write <u>one programming tip</u> that other students might find helpful when they are programming.

_____

_____

_____

_____

_____

Engineer's Two Step Programming Sheet

Engineer: _____ Date: _____

Teammate: _____

Your new programming challenge is: To lift a load to the top of your crane, and then lower back to the ground. This forward and reverse motion requires a two step program.

1. With your teammate discuss the time needed for your carne to lift the load to the top. Estimate the time.

2. Complete the sentence shown below:

   Our crane will lift the load for _____ seconds and then it will lower the load for _____ seconds.

3. Using the icons on the **Programmer's Icon Sheet** cut and paste the icons to plan out your program.

Program 1: Our crane will lift the load for _____ seconds and then it will lower the load for _____ seconds.

4. Now check in with your teacher for instructions on how select this program on your computer. You will be assigned a computer to use.

   - Select "Programmer" when ROBOLAB opens.
   - Double click on "Pilot 3" to open the program.
   - Create the program on the screen by selecting the icons that match the icons on the paper program you created.
   - When finished creating the program, put your RCX next to the IR Tower.
   - Turn your RCX on.
   - Click the big white arrow on Pilot 3 screen.
   - Wait while the program loads on to your RCX.
   - Run your RCX.

5. When you are successful with your time, write a different program with different times.

6. Complete the sentence with your new times:

   Our crane will lift the load for _____ seconds and then it will lower the load for _____ seconds.

7. Reflect on your programming in Pilot 3. How was Pilot 3 different from Pilot 1?

   _____

   _____

   _____

   _____

   _____

8. Write one programming tip that other students might find helpful when they are programming in Pilot 3.

   _____

   _____

   _____

Programmer's Icon Sheet

Cut and paste the icon desired on your Engineering Programming Sheet

Motors:

Forward

Reverse

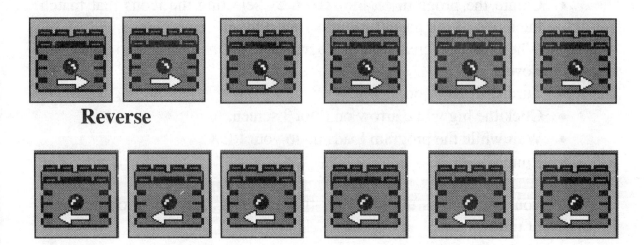

Time:

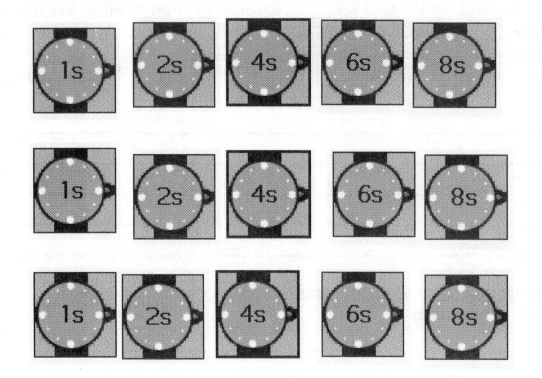

Grade Two
Project Eleven: Learning with Levers

Project Objective: To learn the parts of a lever and how a lever is used to lift a load.

Time: Two to three 45 minute periods

Materials:
- LEGO® Mindstorm or Simple Machine kits
- Centimeter rulers
- Objects to be used for loads (such as blocks, cubes, etc.)
- Objects to be used for fulcrum (such as pencils, etc.)
- Pictures of levers from other sources (such as see saws; pan balance; scissors, nutcrackers, etc.)

Response Sheet:
- Exploring Levers Lesson 1
- Exploring Levers Lesson 2
- Assessment: Levers

Vocabulary:
- Lever
- Load
- Force (or effort)
- Fulcrum
- Work
- Balance

Procedure:

Prior to beginning the project, the teacher should find pictures of levers and bring them class. The project begins with the teacher leading a discussion about levers. The teacher should display different pictures of levers in action. The teacher may ask questions such as:

- Why do people use levers?
- How do levers work?
- What do you think work is?

- How does a lever do work?
- How would you build a lever?

Next, the teacher shows the students a diagram of a lever (Fig. 1) with the new vocabulary building words. He/she defines each word, pointing to it in the picture. The lever is a simple machine used to make work easier. It has some main parts: lever arm, the fulcrum and the load. The lever arm is the bar that moves or pivots when pushed. The fulcrum is the pivot point on the lever. The load is the object being moved by the lever and is located on one end of the lever arm. The applied force is the push or pull exerted on the other end of the lever.

lever   load   force   fulcrum

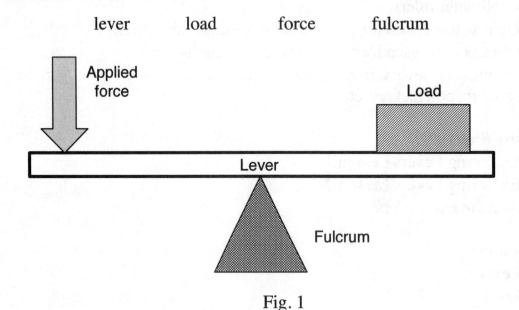

Fig. 1

After teaching the vocabulary on the diagram of the lever, the teacher then displays the pictures of levers. The students identify the different parts of the lever, using the correct word for each part of the lever in the picture.

The teacher then introduces the project. He/she explains that as a team with another student, they will be building and exploring the levers together, completing the Response Sheet as they work. Give each student a Response Sheet: **Exploring Levers Lesson 1**. Review the Response Sheet and answer any questions that the students might have. Students then begin the project. When the student teams finish **Exploring Levers Lesson 1**, the teacher checks their **Response Sheets** for accuracy and completeness. He/she then gives them the next **Response Sheet: Exploring Levers Lesson 2** to complete.

After completing both **Response Sheets**, the teacher leads a class discussion about the project with questions such as:

- What is something new that you learned about levers?
- Have you seen any levers similar to the models you designed and built?
- What was the force you used for moving the lever arm?
- How did you apply this force?

The lever models will be dissembled at the conclusion of the project. Students will be instructed on the care of LEGO® materials and to sort and store the pieces.

The **Lever Assessment** sheet should be distributed at the end of the project.

Extensions:

- Build other models of levers with the fulcrum in different locations.

Assessment:

- Completion of the Response Sheet: **Exploring Levers Lesson 1**.
- Completion of the Response Sheet: **Exploring Levers Lesson 2**.
- Completion of the **Lever Assessment Sheet**
- Teacher observations and interviews

Response Sheet

Exploring Levers: Lesson 1

Engineer: _____ Date: _____

Teammate: _____

Levers for Lifting

A **lever** is a bar that turns about a point when it is pushed or pulled. The point is called the **fulcrum.** The **push** or **pull** is called the **force**. Levers are used to lift heavy **loads.**

1. Build model that looks like the photograph below. We will call this **Test 1**.

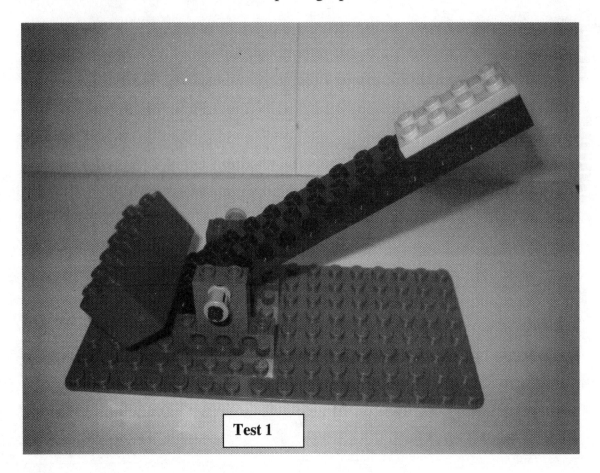

Test 1

2. **Draw and label** the parts of the model.
   Label: the lever, fulcrum, and load. Draw your hand to apply the force.

3. **Press down** on the lever and **feel the force** needed to lift the load.

4. Write down your observations about **Test 1**:

   _____

   _____

   _____

5. Notice how high the load is lifted in **Test 1**. Measure how high it went using the centimeter ruler. Complete the **data table.**

	Height (in cm)
Test 1	

6. Now place the load at the other end of the lever arm by moving the fulcrum as shown in the model presented below. We will call this **Test 2.**

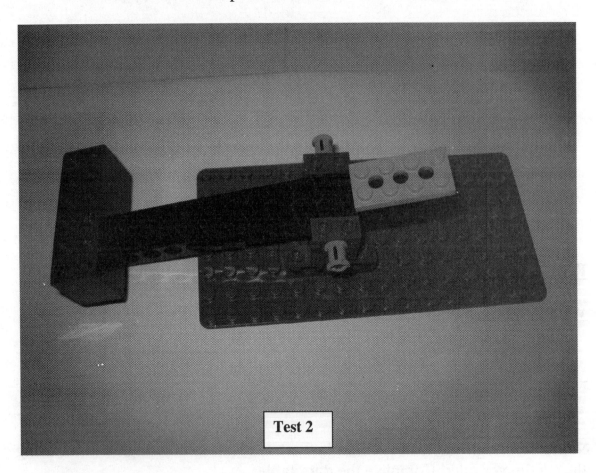

Test 2

7. **Press down** on the lever and **feel the force** needed to lift the load.

8. Describe in writing some observations you about **Test 2**:

_____

_____

_____

9. Notice how high the load is lifted in **Test 2**. Measure how high it went using a **centimeter ruler**. Complete the **data table.**

	Height (in cm)
Test 2	

Think about what you observed with the two models, Test 1 and Test 2.

10. Which lever made it easier to lift a load?
    Test 1   Test 2
    (circle your choice)

Why do you think so?

_____

_____

_____

11. Which lever lifted the load farther? (circle your choice)

      Test 1   Test 2

Why do you think so?

_____

_____

_____

Response Sheet
Exploring Levers: Lesson 2

Engineer: _____ Date: _____

Teammate: _____

Balanced Forces

Balances are levers that move when forces (**push** or **pull**) are applied. The object to be weighed pushes on one side of the lever. The balance pivots on its **fulcrum**. Known weights are placed on the other pan until the lever is level. Balances like this one can be used to measure the weight of an object.

1. Build a model that looks like this. We will call this **Model 1**.

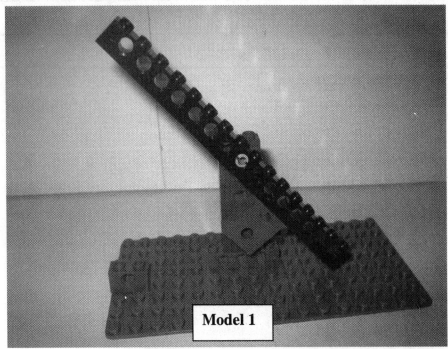

Model 1

front view

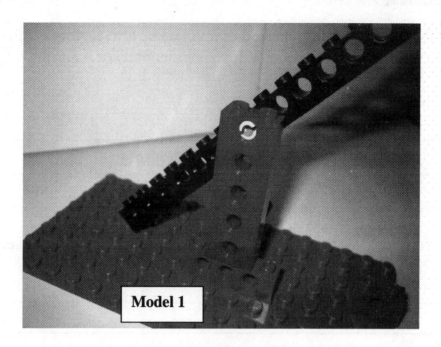

Oblique view of the back side

2. **Draw and label** the parts of the model. Label: lever arm, fulcrum, and load.

3. Write down your observations about **Model 1**:

_____

_____

_____

4. Notice that **Model 1** is **not** balanced or level. The arm (lever) is tilted. What could you do to make this are become level (horizontal) or balanced?

Write down one of your ideas.

_____

_____

_____

5. Now try your idea. What happened? Describe in writing your observations.

_____

_____

6. Change your **Model** 1 to look like the one shown below. We will call this **Model 2**.

Model 2

7. Write down your observations about **Model 2**:

_____

_____

8. Explore **Model 2** trying to find **as many ways** as possible to achieve balance.

9. Draw some of the other ways you balanced **Model 2**. Add more drawing boxes if necessary.

Lever Assessment

Engineer: _____ Date: _____

Simple machines help us do work by trading **distance** for **force**.

Directions: Use the rulers as lever arms, pencils as fulcrums and other objects found in the classroom to serve as loads. Then design an experiment to explain the sentence above.

Here is what I did in my experiment:

I discovered that:

_____

_____

_____

_____

_____

Grade Two
Project Twelve: Build a Catapult

Project Objective: To familiarized the students with levers and build a simple lever system such as a catapult.

Time: Three to four 45 minute periods

Materials:
- LEGO® Mindstorm or Simple Machine kits
- Metric Tape Measure, meter stick or metric rulers
- Metric rulers
- Plastic spoons
- Rubber bands
- Cotton balls
- Masking tape
- Pictures of levers from Project 11
- Lacrosse stick with a soft nerf ball or a picture of a lacrosse stick

Response Sheet:
- Design Sheet: Designing a Catapult
- Catapults- How Far can they throw?
- Extension- Estimating with Catapults
- Reflection- Catapults
- Self Evaluation: Levers

Vocabulary:
- load
- force or effort
- fulcrum
- catapult
- trebuchet

Procedure:

The project begins with the teacher leading a discussion reviewing levers. The teacher displays different pictures of levers from the previous lesson and reviews the vocabulary associated with levers: lever arm, load, force and fulcrum. The teacher may ask questions such as:

- Where is the fulcrum in this picture?
- What load is being lifted in this picture?
- Where is the force in the picture?
- What is the work this lever does?
- Why do people use levers?
- How do levers work?

The teacher then displays the lacrosse stick, or a picture of the stick, and asks the class if anyone knows what the use of this piece of sporting equipment. The class discusses the lacrosse stick and how it is used. If a lacrosse stick is available, the teacher models how the stick works by flinging the nerf ball across the room. He/she asks the students to identify the different parts of the lever on the stick: the lever arm (the stick itself); the load flung (the nerf ball); the fulcrum (the players wrist); and the force (the push by the arm). The teacher then identifies the lacrosse stick as a catapult, or a type of lever used for flinging objects such as balls.

The students are presented with the building project, which is to build a catapult that can fling a cotton ball using its lever arm. The cotton ball must be thrown at least 25 centimeters from the catapult. The teacher holds up metric ruler and shows the class a distance of 25 centimeters on the ruler. The teacher instructs the students that the catapults **must only throw cotton balls** because of safety issues. It is important to keep everyone safe in the classroom. Catapulting heavier objects is dangerous! The teacher should discuss the safety issues with this rule.

The teacher asks the students what types fulcrums they might use to build their catapults, and discusses the properties of a fulcrum that make it better able to fling a cotton ball. Topics include:

- Ability to move or rotate
- Sturdy
- Ability to support the lever arm.

The teacher instructs the class that they will have a variety of materials to use in addition to the LEGOs to build their catapult. The teacher displays the materials as he/she introduces them. These materials include LEGO® building pieces, masking tape, plastic spoons and rubber bands.

The students are divided into teams of two and given the **Design Sheet: Designing a Catapult**. The teacher discusses the sheet with the students. The teams are instructed to discuss their ideas together and draw a catapult that they might build using the LEGO® pieces and the other materials. The teams should check with the teacher to obtain his/her approval before they begin to build their catapult.

As each team finishes building their catapult, they are given a copy of the **Response Sheet: Testing Catapults: How far can they throw?** The team is instructed to use their catapult and test its throwing power. The teacher should discuss the sheet with each team, demonstrating how to measure the distance traveled by the cotton ball. The teacher shows the students how to find the average of three tests.

When all teams have completed their testing and have recorded their data, the teacher brings the class together so that each team can share their catapults. The teacher asks each team to introduce the catapult, report on its maximum throwing distance and then show how the catapult works. The teacher asks each team to share a building problem they encountered and describe to the class their solution to the problem. The Response **Sheets Catapult Reflection and Self Evaluation: Levers** should be distributed at the conclusion of the project.

If possible, the catapults should be displayed for the school community to view. They can then be disassembled at a convenient time. Students will be instructed on the care of the LEGO® materials and in sorting and storing them.

Extensions:

- Students redesign catapult to throw farther and to complete the **Response Sheet Extension- Estimating with Catapults.**
- Students redesign catapult to have a cotton ball holder .

Assessment:

- Successful building of a working model of a catapult
- Completion of the Design Sheet: **Designing A Catapult**
- Completion of the Response Sheet: **Catapults: How Far can they throw?**
- Completion of the Response Sheet: **Reflection: Catapults**
- Teacher observations and interviews

Examples of student engineered catapults

A trebuchet

Testing

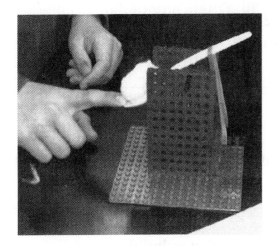

Rubber band increases force

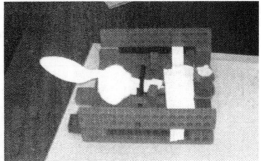

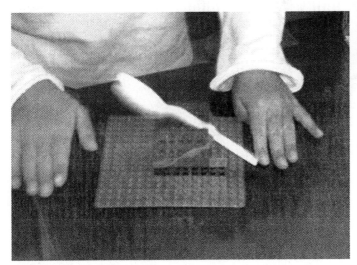

Design Sheet
Designing a Catapult

Engineer: _____Date: _____

Teammate: _____

1. With your partner, discuss some ideas you have about designing and building your catapult.

    *   Use ideas from both teammates.
    *   Prepare a drawing of your design that you plan to build.

2. Describe your design in writing:

_____

_____

_____

_____

_____

_____

Response Sheet
Catapults: How far can they throw?

Engineer: _____Date: _____

Teammate: _____

1. Test your catapult to see how far it can throw the cotton ball. Measure the distance the cotton ball travels using a tape measure. Record the distance on the data table.

Name of Catapult: _____

First time testing	Distance (cm)
#1	
#2	
#3	
Average	

2. What could you do to your catapult's design to make the cotton ball go even farther?

_____

_____

_____

3. Try it.

4. Retest your catapult to see how far it can throw the cotton ball. Measure the distance the cotton ball travels using a tape measure. Record the distance on the data table.

Second time testing	Distance (cm)
#1	
#2	
#3	
Average	

Response Sheet
Extension: Estimating with Catapults

Engineer: _____ Date: _____

Teammate: _____

1. Does the length of the throwing arm of the catapult make a difference in how far the cotton ball goes? Write a hypothesis about what you think.

   _____

   _____

2. Design an experiment to test your hypothesis. Write what you will do.

   _____

   _____

   _____

   _____

3. Now test your catapult's throwing arm. Complete the data table, changing the arm length with each test.

Length of arm (cm)	Distance (cm)

4. Use a piece of graph paper and create a point-line graph of your data table.

5. Using your graph, answer these questions. Describe the shape of your graph.

   _____

   _____

   _____

6. Estimate the distance a ball would travel for a length of arm that is not on your graph.

       Length of arm   _____cm
       Estimate of distance   _____cm

7. Describe how you used the graph to estimate this distance.

_____

_____

_____

_____

_____

8. Test your catapult throwing arm for that length of arm not on your graph.

- What distance did you determine? _____cm

- Was this the same or different as your answer to question 6? _____

- Why do you think this happened?

_____

_____

_____

_____

_____

Response Sheet
Reflection: Catapults

Engineer: _____ Date: _____

Teammate: _____

1. Prepare a drawing of the catapult you built:

2. Examine the picture you drew at the beginning of this project. Reflect on how it is different from what you built. Discuss in writing some of your thoughts.

_____

_____

_____

3. Reflect on your building. Why did you build your catapult differently from what you originally thought you would build?

_____

_____

_____

Appendix A: Alignment with the National Science Education Standards for the United States

The engineering activities in this book have been aligned to the National Science Educational Standards for the United States for Kindergarten through Grade Four. The National Science Educational Standards goal are to promote science literacy for all students, Kindergarten through Grade 12, by summarizing habits of mind necessary for science inquiry as well as learning standards of science understanding.

Inquiry is the basis for this series of lessons in which students construct knowledge of science and engineering through experiential learning. Using the LEGO® materials, students actively engage in exploring the material, asking questions, constructing models or prototypes and testing their designs. Students modify their designs based on knowledge learned though observations of the models. Knowledge is constructed over the series of lessons all of which build on concepts covered in previous lessons. The engineer lessons and materials provide a powerful, authentic way for students to actively engage in scientific thinking.

The tables list the standards covered by each project by each grade level. The "X" in the box indicated that that standard is addressed in the project listed in the row.

Alignment with the National Science Standards, Grades K-2

Content Standards

Kindergarten Projects	Develop abilities necessary to do scientific inquiry	Develop understanding about scientific inquiry	Properties of objects and materials	Position and motion of objects	Abilities of technological design	Understanding about science and technology	Abilities to distinguish between natural objects and objects made by humans	Science and technology in local challenges	Science as a human endeavor
Project One: Introduction to Engineering and LEGO® Building	X		X			X			
Project Two: Building with a Fixed Number of LEGO® Pieces	X								
Project Three: Spinners	X	X		X					
Project Four: Lifting a Load	X			X		X		X	
Project Five: Balance	X			X				X	
Project Six: Catching the Wind	X	X	X	X	X	X	X		X

Content Standards

Grade One Projects	Develop abilities necessary to do scientific inquiry	Develop understanding about scientific inquiry	Properties of objects and materials	Position and motion of objects	Abilities of technological design	Understanding about science and technology	Abilities to distinguish between natural objects and objects made by humans	Science and technology in local challenges	Science as a human endeavor
Project One: Introduction to LEGOs	X		X						
Project Two: Introduction to Plates, Axles and Tires	X		X						
Project Three: Build a Sturdy Wall	X			X		X			
Project Four: Build a Chair for Mr. Bear	X	X		X	X	X			
Project Five: Introduction to Gears	X					X			
Project Six: Introduction to Pulleys	X			X		X		X	
Project Seven: Introduction to Motors	X					X		X	
Project Eight: Build a Car	X	X		X	X		X	X	X
Project Nine: Build a Snowplow	X	X		X	X	X	X	X	X

Content Standards

Grade Two Projects	Develop abilities necessary to do scientific inquiry	Develop understanding about scientific inquiry	Properties of objects and materials	Position and motion of objects	Abilities of technological design	Understanding about science and technology	Abilities to distinguish between natural objects and objects made by humans	Science and technology in local challenges	Science as a human endeavor
Project One: Introduction to LEGO® Building	X		X						
Project Two: Wheel and Axle	X	X	X	X		X	X		
Project Three: Gears	X		X			X			
Project Four: Crown Gears	X					X			
Project Five: Worm Gears	X								X
Project Six: Motorizing Tractor	X	X		X			X		X
Project Seven: A Snail Robot	X	X		X	X		X		X
Project Eight: Pulley Power	X		X	X					X
Project Nine: Building a Crane	X			X		X	X	X	X
Project Ten: Motorize a Crane	X	X		X			X	X	X
Project Eleven: Learning with Levers			X	X		X			X
Project Twelve: Build a Catapult		X		X	X	X	X	X	X

Appendix B

Activities Listed by Topic

Balance

- Kindergarten Project Five: Balance
- Grade Two Project Eleven: Learning with Levers
- Grade Two Project Twelve: Build a Catapult

Engineering Design Process

- Kindergarten Project Six: Catching the Wind
- Grade One Project Nine: Build a Snowplow
- Grade Two Project Seven: Snail Robot
- Grade Two Project Twelve: Build a Catapult

Forces

- Grade One Project Eight: Build a Car
- Grade Two Project Twelve: Build a Catapult

Friction

- Kindergarten Project Six: Catching the Wind
- Grade One Project Eight: Build a Car
- Grade Two Project Two: Wheel and Axle

Gears

- Kindergarten Project Three: Spinners
- Grade One Project Five: Introduction to Gears
- Grade Two Project Three: Gears

- Grade Two Project Six: Introduction to Pulleys
- Grade Two Project Seven: Snail Robot

Graphing

- Grade Two Project Seven: Snail Robot

Levers

- Kindergarten Project Five: Balance
- Grade Two Project Eleven: Learning with Levers
- Grade Two Project Twelve: Build a Catapult

Mathematics

- Kindergarten Project Two: Building with a Fixed Number of Pieces
- Kindergarten Project Five: Balance
- Grade One Project One: Introduction to LEGO®'s
- Grade One Project Two: Introduction to Plates, Axles and Tires
- Grade One Project Three: Build a Sturdy Wall
- Grade One Project Four: Build a Chair for Mr. Bear
- Grade One Project Five: Introduction to Gears
- Grade Two Project Three: Gears
- Grade Two Project Five: Worm Gears
- Grade Two Project Seven: A Snail Robot
- Grade Two Project Ten: Motorize a Crane

Mathematics (Continued)

- Grade Two Project Eleven: Learning with Levers
- Grade Two Project Twelve: Build a Catapult

Measuring Tools

- Grade One Project Two: Introduction to Plates, Axles and Tires
- Grade One Project Four: Build a Chair for Mr. Bear
- Grade Two Project Seven: Snail Robot
- Grade Two Project Eleven: Learning with Levers
- Grade Two Project Twelve: Build a Catapult

Position and Motion of Objects

- Kindergarten Project Five: Balance
- Grade One Project Five: Introduction to Gears
- Grade One Project Six: Introduction to Pulleys
- Grade One Project Seven: Introduction to Motors
- Grade One Project Nine: Build a Snowplow
- Grade Two Project Three: Gears
- Grade Two Project Four: Crown Gears
- Grade Two Project Eight: Pulley Power
- Grade Two Project Eleven: Learning with Levers
- Grade Two Project Twelve: Build a Catapult

Properties of Objects

- Kindergarten Project One: Introduction to Engineering and LEGO® Building
- Kindergarten Project Six: Catching the Wind
- Grade One Project One: Introduction to LEGO® s
- Grade One Project Two: Introduction to Plates, Axles and Tires
- Grade Two Project One: Introduction to LEGO® Building
- Grade Two Project Two: Wheel and Axle
- Grade Two Project Three: Gears
- Grade Two Project Eight: Pulley Power
- Grade Two Project Eleven: Learning with Levers

Pulleys

- Kindergarten Project Four: Lifting a Load
- Grade One Project Six: Introduction to Pulleys
- Grade One Project Eight: Build a Car
- Grade Two Project Eight: Pulley Power
- Grade Two Project Nine: Building a Crane
- Grade Two Project Ten: Motorize a Crane

Simple Machines

- Kindergarten Project Three: Spinners
- Kindergarten Project Four: Lifting a Load

Simple Machines (Continued)

- Kindergarten Project Five: Balance
- Grade One Project Five: Introduction to Gears
- Grade One Project Six: Introduction to Pulleys
- Grade One Project Eight: Build a Car
- Grade Two Project Two: Wheel and Axle
- Grade Two Project Three: Gears
- Grade Two Project Seven: Snail Robot
- Grade Two Project Eight: Pulley Power
- Grade Two Project Eleven: Learning with Levers
- Grade Two Project Twelve: Build a Catapult

Stability

- Kindergarten Project Five: Balance
- Grade One Project Three: Build a Sturdy Wall
- Grade One Project Four: Build a Chair for Mr. Bear
- Grade Two Project Twelve: Build a Catapult

Wheel and Axle

- Kindergarten Project Six: Catching the Wind
- Grade One Project Two: Introduction to Plates, Axles and Tires
- Grade One Project Eight: Build a Car
- Grade Two Project Two: Wheel and Axle

Appendix C

Equipment Used for Each Project

Kindergarten Projects	Duplos	LEGOs	Motors	Battery Pack	RCX
Kindergarten Project One: Introduction to Engineering and LEGO® Building	X				
Kindergarten Project Two: Building with a Fixed Number of LEGO® Pieces	X				
Kindergarten Project Three: Spinners	X				
Kindergarten Project Four: Lifting a Load	X				
Kindergarten Project Five: Balance	X				

Grade One Projects	Duplos	LEGOs	Motors	Battery Pack	RCX
Grade One Project One: Introduction to LEGOs		X			
Grade One Project Two: Introduction to Plates, Axles and Tire		X			
Grade One Project Three: Build a Sturdy Wall		X			
Grade One Project Four: Build a Chair for Mr. Bear		X			
Grade One Project Five: Introduction to Gears		X			
Grade One Project Six: Introduction to Pulleys		X			
Grade One Project Seven: Introduction to Motors		X	X	X	X
Grade One Project Eight: Build a Car		X	X	X	X
Grade One Project Nine: Build a Snowplow		X	X	X	X

Grade Two Projects	Duplos	LEGOs	Motors	Battery Pack	RCX
Grade Two Project One: Introduction to LEGO® Building		X			
Grade Two Project Two: Wheel and Axle		X			
Grade Two Project Three: Gears		X			
Grade Two Project Four: Crown Gears		X			
Grade Two Project Five: Worm Gears		X		X	X
Grade Two Project Six: Motorizing the Tractor		X	X	X	X
Grade Two Project Seven: A Snail Robot		X	X		X
Grade Two Project Eight: Pulley Power		X			
Grade Two Project Nine: Building a Crane		X			X
Grade Two Project Ten: Motorize a Crane		X	X		X
Grade Two Project Eleven: Learning with Levers		X			
Grade Two Project Twelve: Build a Catapult		X			